IS THE BIBLE TRUE?
SEVEN ADDRESSES

JAMES H. BROOKES

ALICIA EDITIONS

CONTENTS

Preface	v
1. INSPIRATION	1
2. THE CANON OF THE NEW TESTAMENT	19
3. THE CHARACTER OF JESUS	37
4. HUMAN ESTIMATE OF JESUS	57
5. THE RESURRECTION OF JESUS	77
6. THE BIBLE ITS OWN WITNESS	99
7. ALLEGED CONTRADICTIONS	119

PREFACE

Certain gentlemen of culture and influence requested an answer to the leading arguments which Strauss, in his Life of Jesus, urges against the credibility of the Gospel history. This accounts for the frequent allusions in the following pages to the celebrated German skeptic. Of course every intelligent Christian has learned, perhaps by experience, the fruitlessness of a mere intellectual combat with infidelity; but the request could not have been declined without dishonor to the Master.

The answer was given on seven successive evenings of the Lord's day; and several believers who heard the discourses have desired their publication, hoping that they may be helpful and suggestive to some of the Lord's little ones, by presenting in a brief and cheap form a few facts and thoughts, which prove the Bible to be more than the work of man.

These friends know that the Lectures were written under the burden of manifold labors, and that during the entire period always eight, and generally ten, public services claimed attention each week, besides other cares it would be improper to mention here. Only a few hours, snatched from various engagements, could be devoted to their preparation, and there was no opportunity to revise even one of them at leisure.

They are sent forth, therefore, with a humiliating consciousness of their failure to present, in any proper clearness and fulness, the claims of Jesus and His word. But He knows that they were gladly undertaken solely for Him; and now as a most imperfect offering they are laid at His feet with the prayer, that He may be pleased to use the weak things of the world to confound the things which are mighty.

James H. Brookes

CHAPTER I
INSPIRATION

Strauss says in his Preface to the Life of Jesus, "What we especially want to know is this:—is the Gospel history true and reliable as a whole, and in its details, or is it not?" This is indeed precisely what we want to know, and what it greatly concerns us to know, for if the Gospel history is true and reliable, not only as a whole, but in its details, it is obvious that the destiny of the soul turns upon our acceptance or rejection of its testimony. "He that believeth on the Son hath everlasting life: and he that believeth not the Son shall not see life; but the wrath of God abideth on him;" "Then said Jesus again unto them, I go my way, and ye shall seek me, and shall die in your sins: whither I go, ye can not come. Then said the Jews, will he kill himself! because he saith. Whither I go, ye can not come. And he said unto them. Ye are from beneath; I am from above: ye are of this world; I am not of this world. I said therefore unto you, that ye shall die in your sins: for if ye believe not that I am he, ye shall die in your sins," (John iii. 36; viii. 21-24).

Let us, then, with all the interest which the momentous importance of the subject demands, and with all the fairness of a calm and dispassionate examination, take up the question presented by Strauss. If it can be shown that the Gospel history has a divine and imperative claim upon our belief, no honest man will reject that claim, however humbling to his pride of intellect, however sharp the conviction it brings that he needs a mighty Saviour to deliver him from ruin, however complete the revolution it demands of his opinions, habits, and associations. If, on the other hand, an impartial and thorough investigation of the subject proves that the New Testament narrative is not worthy of credit, as a whole, or in its details, we must dismiss all thought of a revelation from God other than the displays of His greatness and glory in the works of creation, and be guided by the dim glimmerings of the human mind through the labyrinth of life, or resign ourselves to our dark and inexplicable fate. Nothing more is asked now than a response to the reasonable request of Joshua and of Elijah: "If it seem evil unto you to serve the Lord, choose you this day whom ye will serve:" "How long halt ye between two opinions? if the Lord be God, follow him: but if Baal, then follow him," (Josh. xxiv. 15; 1 Kings xviii. 21).

None will deny that it is proper to begin our research with the inquiry, what does the Bible say of itself, or what do its writers affirm of its authority? Of course no attempt will be made to prove to a skeptic its inspiration by its own testimony; but even the skeptic will wish to know with what pretensions it comes to us, and whether it asserts that it is only of human origin, or insists that it contains the very word of God. We find that it embraces sixty-six separate books, written at various intervals during a period of about sixteen hundred years, or, as some modern infidels think, a still longer period. It professes to treat of the entire term of man's existence upon the earth, from his creation to the judgment of the great white throne at the close of a thousand years of millennial peace and righteousness. Its authors were of various occupations, as lawgivers, generals, judges, kings, priests, governors, farmers, shepherds, herdmen, fishermen, soldiers, physicians, and tax-gatherers; including every variety of intellectual endowment, and literary attainment, and social position.

Opening this remarkable volume, so unlike any other, we read the equally remarkable statement, "ALL scripture is given by inspiration of God, and is profitable for doctrine, for reproof, for correction, for instruction in righteousness; that the man of God may be perfect, thoroughly furnished unto all good works," (2 Tim. iii. 16, 17). The scripture to which reference is here made, as shown in the preceding verse, is contained in the Old Testament, known by Timothy from his childhood, and able, it is added, to make him wise unto salvation through faith which is in Christ Jesus. The scripture is literally *writing*, and a writing consists of letters and words, not merely of thoughts. What is WRITTEN, therefore, is declared to be inspired of God, and that which is inspired of God is "ALL SCRIPTURE," embracing all that is written. Or if the sentence should be rendered, as some prefer, "every scripture inspired of God is profitable," this only imparts stronger force to the declaration; for it then links itself to the sacred writings mentioned just before, and affirms of every one of these that it is given by inspiration of God.

"For the prophecy came not in old time [or at any time, as it is in the margin] by the will of man: but holy men of God spake as they were moved by the Holy Ghost," (2 Pet. i. 21). A careful examination of the terms *prophecy* and *prophet* as employed in the Bible will show that they are not to be limited to the prediction of future events, but prophecy is the revelation of the mind of God in human language, and a prophet is one who utters the words of God, whether they refer to that which is past or yet to come, to doctrine or to duty. Here then it is distinctly asserted that the revelation of God's pleasure and purpose concerning Himself, or concerning His people, or concerning the world at large, came not of old time by the will of man; but holy men of God SPAKE, not thought simply, as they were moved by the Holy Ghost.

Turning to these men of old time we find David, for example, testifying on his dying bed, "The Spirit of the Lord SPAKE by me, and his WORD [not His thought only] was in my tongue," (2 Sam. xxiii. 2). Isaiah opens his prophecy by saying, "Hear the word of the Lord," (Isa. i. 10), and twenty times does he declare that his writing was the WORD, not the thought simply, of the Lord. Jeremiah begins by saying, "The word of the Lord came unto me," (Jer. i. 4), and nearly one hundred times does he use this form of expression, or declare that he was uttering the word of the Lord, and the word of the living God. Ezekiel begins by saying, "The word of the Lord came expressly unto Ezekiel the priest," (Ezek. i. 3); "Son of man all my words that I shall speak unto thee receive in thine heart—and tell them, Thus saith the Lord God," (Ezek. iii. 10, 11); and about sixty times in his prophecy he repeats the assertion or its equivalent, announcing that his statements, both as a whole, and in all their details, were to be accepted as the very words of God.

Daniel says, "I Daniel understood by books the number of the years, whereof the word of the Lord came to Jeremiah the prophet, that he would accomplish seventy years in the desolations of Jerusalem," (Dan. ix. 2); "and when I heard the voice of his words, then was I in a deep sleep on my face, and my face to the ground," (Dan. x. 9). Hosea says,

"The word of the Lord that came unto Hosea," (Hosea i. 1); Joel says, "The word of the Lord that came to Joel," (Joel i. 1); Amos says, "Hear this word that the Lord hath spoken against you," (Amos iii. 1; Obadiah says, "Thus saith the Lord God," (Oba. i. 1); Jonah says, "The word of the Lord came unto Jonah," (Jon. i. 1); Micah says, "The word of the Lord that came to Micah," (Mic. i. 1); Nahum says, "Thus saith the Lord," (Na. i. 12); Habakkuk says, "The Lord answered me, and said," (Hab. ii. 2); Zephaniah says, "The word of the Lord which came unto Zephaniah," (Zep. i. 1); Haggai says, "In the sixth month, in the first day of the month, came the word of the Lord by Haggai the prophet," (Hag. i. 1); Zechariah says, "In the eighth month, in the second year of Darius, came the word of the Lord unto Zechariah," (Zec. i. 1); Malachi says, "The burden of the word of the Lord to Israel by Malachi," (Mal. i. 1).

Thus do all the writers of old time, who are specially classed as prophets, solemnly affirm without a single exception that the very words contained in their writings are the words of Jehovah. Several hundred years elapsed between the first and the last of these prophets; but in hundreds of instances, and with unvarying testimony, do they declare that they were uttering the words of God, not their own words, in their manifold communications to men. In no instance do they intimate that some of the words they used were suggested by themselves, or learned from human authority, or mingled with the words which God put into their mouths; but they uniformly insist that they were repeating the words of the Lord. One of the latest of them says of his unbelieving countrymen, "They made their hearts as an adamant stone, lest they should hear the law, and the words which the Lord of hosts sent in his Spirit by the former prophets," (Zec. vii. 12); and the very latest of them twenty-four times in four brief chapters uses the expression, "THUS SAITH THE LORD."

Nor is the expression by any means confined to the writers particularly distinguished as prophets. It is of constant occurrence in the five books of Moses, in the books known as historical, and in the books included under the general title of the Psalms. In hundreds upon hundreds of verses as any one can easily see by glancing at a good Concordance, we read, "Thus saith the Lord," "The Lord said," "The Lord spake," "The Lord hath spoken," "The Lord promised," "The saying of the Lord," "The word of the Lord;" and thus all the writers of the Old Testament at least claim that the language they used was not their own, but the very language which God commanded them to utter. They do not give the slightest recognition to a doctrine unknown to the Christian Church for a thousand years, an invention of modern times to please infidelity, by which it is supposed that only their thoughts were inspired, or that they were only partially inspired, or that their inspiration was not in equal degree to all, or that they had at one time an inspiration of supervision, at another an inspiration of elevation, at another an inspiration of direction; but they stand or fall upon the bold statement that the words they spoke and wrote were precisely the words God told them to write and speak.

Not only so, but they assure us that men were sometimes forced to utter the words the Lord put into their mouths, when they were unwilling to do His bidding, or unconscious of the scope and significance of their deliverances, or even opposed to the very testimony they were compelled to bear. Thus Moses recoiled from the divine command to stand before the king of Egypt in behalf of the oppressed Hebrews, and exclaimed in his distress, "O my Lord, I am not eloquent, neither heretofore, nor since thou hast spoken unto thy servant: but I am slow of speech, and of a slow tongue. And the Lord said onto him, Who hath made man's mouth? or who maketh the dumb, or deaf, or the seeing, or the blind? have not I the Lord"? How therefore go, and I will be with thy mouth, and teach thee what thou shalt say," (Ex. iv. 10-12).

"Baalam the son of Bosor, who loved the wages of unrighteousness; but was rebuked for his iniquity: the dumb ass, speaking with man's voice, forbad the madness of the prophet," (2 Pet. ii. 15,16), said to Balak, "Lo, I am come unto thee: have I now any power at all to say anything? the word that God putteth in my mouth, that shall I speak." Again and again he sought to curse the Israelites, but each time a blessing fell from his lips; and when at length Balak said, "Neither curse them at all, nor bless them at all," Balaam answered, "Told not I thee, saying, All that the Lord speaketh, that I must do?" (Num. xxii. 38; xxiii. 26).

"Saul sent messengers to take David: and when they saw the company of the prophets prophesying, and Samuel standing as appointed over them, the Spirit of God was upon the messengers of Saul, and they also prophesied. And when it was told Saul, lie sent other messengers, and they prophesied, likewise. And Saul sent messengers again the third time, and they prophesied also." Then Saul himself determined to go, "and the Spirit of God was upon him also, and he went on, and prophesied until he came to Naioth in Eamah. And he stripped off his clothes also, and prophesied before Samuel in like manner, and lay down naked all that day, and all that night. Wherefore they say, Is Saul also among the prophets?" (1 Sam. xix. 20-24).

A prophet of Israel invited to his house a prophet of Judah, and while his guest was seated at his table the word of the Lord came unto him and he suddenly cried out, "Thus saith the Lord, Forasmuch as thou hast disobeyed the mouth of the Lord, and hast not kept the commandment which the Lord thy God commanded thee, but camest back, and hast eaten bread and drunk water in the place of the which the LORD did say to thee, Eat no bread, and drink no water; thy carcase shall not come unto the sepulchre of thy fathers, (1 Kings xiii. 21, 22).

Jeremiah, when informed by the word of the Lord that he was sanctified from his birth and ordained to be a prophet unto the nations, timidly answered, "Ah! Lord God! behold, I can not speak; for I am a child. But the Lord said unto me, Say not, I am a child: for thou shalt go to all that I shall send thee; and whatsoever I command thee thou shalt speak. Be not afraid of their faces: for I am with thee to deliver thee, saith the Lord. Then the Lord put forth his hand, and touched my mouth. And the Lord said unto me, Behold, I have put my words in thy mouth," (Jer. i. 6-9).

Caiaphas, who is introduced to us in the gospel of John as high priest of the Jews at the time of Christ's crucifixion, said to the Council, "Ye know nothing at all, nor consider that it is expedient for us, that one man should die for the people, and that the whole nation perish not. *And this spake he not of himself*: but being high priest that year, he prophesied that Jesus should die for that nation; And not for that nation only, but also that he should gather together in one the children of God that were scattered abroad," (John xi. 49-52).

These illustrations, which could be readily increased, are sufficient to show that the writers of the Bible affirm the existence of an inspiration not merely complete and verbal, but an inspiration that soared entirely above the human mind, that often thwarted the human will, and that frequently put into the human mouth words, the meaning of which was wholly unknown to the person who uttered them. Such is the inspiration brought to view from the first of Genesis to the last of Malachi; nor is there a hint that only part of these ancient writings is inspired, or that they are inspired in different degrees. The theory now too commonly held among those professing to be Christians, that we are to look for a partial and variable inspiration in the Scriptures, is a device of man's intellect in these "latter times;" and is never mentioned by the inspired penmen themselves, who in numberless instances represent their relation to the book as that of Amanuenses writing at the dictation of a master.

Let us now turn to the New Testament for a moment to see what it says of the holy men of God who "spake as they were moved by the Holy Ghost." Scarcely have we opened it before we read, "Now all this was done, that it might be fulfilled which was spoken of the Lord by the prophet," literally, "by the Lord through the prophet," (Matt. i. 22). The same form of expression frequently occurs, as in Matt. ii. 5, 15, 23; iv. 14; viii. 17; xii. 17; xiii. 35; xxi. 4; xxii. 31; and it always points to God as the source of the declaration that is quoted, and to the prophet as the mere instrument through which it is communicated. When Jesus referred to the Old Testament scriptures He described them as the "Word of God," and declared that "David himself said by the Holy Ghost," (Mark vii. 13; xii. 36). The phrase, "the Scriptures "occurs fifty times in the New Testament and fifty times it is applied exclusively to the books of the two Testaments, showing that the canon was already announced by the sacred writers. They are also called "the oracles of God," and the "lively [or living] oracles of God," (Rom. iii. 2; Acts. vii. 38). As the derivation of the word *oracle* implies, it is something spoken; and to those who are familiar with the history of the ancient oracles, no term could be employed to set forth more distinctly and positively the plenary inspiration of the Bible, extending to all its language. Over and over through the four Gospels and the Epistles do we find the phrase "God said," or the "Lord said by such a prophet," or the "Holy Ghost said."

As we advance to notice more clearly how the Apostles regarded the ancient scriptures, we have scarcely opened the book containing their Acts when we find Peter saying, "Men and brethren, this scripture must needs have been fulfilled, which the Holy Ghost by the mouth of David spake concerning Judas," (Acts i. 16). Here it is said that it was the Holy Ghost who spake, but by or through the mouth of David. In the next chapter we are told the Apostles "were all filled with the Holy Ghost, and began to speak with other tongues, as the Spirit gave them utterance," (Acts ii. 4), speaking indeed languages with which they had no previous acquaintance, and showing conclusively the nature of inspiration, as extending to the words that were uttered. Afterward, "they lifted up their voice to God with one accord, and said. Lord, thou art God, which hast made heaven, and earth, and the sea, and all that in them is; who by the mouth of thy servant David hast said. Why did the heathen rage, and the people imagine vain things?" (Acts iv. 24, 25).

But it is needless to multiply quotations of this kind, when the most cursory reading of the New Testament will show that its writers invariably refer to the Old Testament as containing the very word of God. The former is quoted in the latter three hundred times, besides numerous allusions to various passages, and it is always mentioned with the reverence due to the immediate communications of Jehovah's mind and will. The men who were employed to write it are regarded as mere instruments engaged by the sovereign pleasure of a higher power, and not only its thoughts, but its words, and all of its words, or all that was written, Jesus Christ and the Apostles directly ascribe to God, without once intimating a partial, varying, or incomplete inspiration. Hence with them the Old Testament was armed with supreme authority, and its testimony was received as if the voice of the Almighty had just spoken in audible accents. The very doctrines at which infidelity has always cavilled, as a personal devil, the depravity of the human heart, everlasting punishment, the need of cleansing blood, the necessity of faith, and the very narratives at which it has sneered, as the destruction of Sodom and Gomorrah, and the history of Jonah, are precisely those upon which Jesus placed the sanction of His own endorsement, willing to link His word and veracity to the word and veracity of the Old Testament, whatever the result.

It will not detain us long to determine the character of the inspiration claimed by the writers of the New Testament. As the Master sent forth His disciples for the first time to preach the kingdom of God to the Jews, He said to them, "When they deliver you up, take no thought how or what ye shall speak; for it shall be given you in that same hour what ye shall speak. For it is not ye that speak, but the Spirit of your Father which speaketh in you," (Matt. x. 19, 20). Still later, standing in the presence of assembled thousands, He said to His followers, "When they bring you into the synagogues, and unto magistrates, and powers, take ye no thought how or what thing ye shall answer, or what ye shall say: for the Holy Ghost shall teach you in the same hour what ye ought to say," (Luke xii. 11, 12). Later still in uttering His last woe against Jerusalem He said to them, "When they shall lead you, and deliver you up, take no thought beforehand what ye shall speak, neither do ye premeditate; but whatsoever shall be given you in that hour, that speak ye: for it is not ye that speak, but the Holy Ghost," (Mark xiii. 11); "Settle it therefore in your hearts, not to meditate before what ye shall answer: for I will give you a mouth and wisdom, which all your adversaries shall not be able to gainsay nor resist," (Luke xxi. 14, 15). Here then is the distinct promise, not only that they should speak with resistless wisdom, but that He would give them a mouth, or put words into their mouth; for it was not they who should speak, but the Holy Ghost.

Accordingly, Luke the beloved Physician, who was not an Apostle, but the travelling companion of Paul, is careful to inform us at the beginning of the gospel which is called by his name, that his knowledge of the events he is about to relate he received from above. "It seemed good to me also, having had perfect understanding of all things from the very first, to write unto thee in order, most excellent Theophilus, that thou mightest know the certainty of those things wherein thou hast been instructed," (Luke i. 3, 4). Here the words *from the very first* ought to have been translated *from above* as it is the same word found in the passage, "the veil of the temple was rent in twain, from the top [or from above] to the bottom," (Matt, xxvii. 51); the same word found in the passage, "He that Cometh from above is above all," (John iii. 31); the same word found in the passage, "Every good gift and every perfect gift is *from above*," (James i. 17); "This wisdom descendeth not *from above*," (James iii. 15); "the wisdom that is *from above* is first pure," (James iii. 17). He had a perfect understanding, then, of all things *from above*, or He wrote as he was moved by the Holy Ghost, that we might know the certainty of those things in which we have been instructed as Christians.

But even if the reading of the English Bible is retained, none will deny the claim of inspiration by Paul with whom he journeyed, and with whose assent and sanction, in connection with the other Apostles, his gospel was sent forth, and the whole canon of the New Testament scriptures was formed. Luke declares it was God who "spake by the mouth of his holy prophets, which have been since the world began," (Luke i. 70); and Paul does not hesitate to place himself in the rank of these holy prophets through whose mouth God spake. Nay, he occupies a higher position, in so far as he is made the channel for the communication of an advanced truth, that was not revealed to the earlier prophets. Writing to the Ephesians he tells "of the grace of God, which is given me to you-ward: how that by revelation he made known unto me the mystery; (as I wrote afore in few words, whereby, when ye read, ye may understand my knowledge in the mystery of Christ;) which in other ages was not made known unto the sons of men, as it is now revealed unto his holy apostles and prophets by the Spirit; that the Gentiles should be fellow-heirs, and of the same body, and partakers of his promise in Christ by the gospel; whereof I was made a minister, according to the gift of the grace of God given unto me by the effectual working of his power," (Eph. iii. 2-7).

Yet in this very passage, in which he quietly declares that he is standing beyond the prophets of old time who spake as they were moved by the Holy Ghost, he also says, "*Unto me who am less than the least of all saints*, is this grace given, that I should preach among the Gentiles the unsearchable riches of Christ," (Eph. iii. 8). In another place he says, "I am the least of the apostles, that am not meet to be called an apostle, because I persecuted the church of God," (1 Cor. xv. 9); and in still another, he exclaims with emotions of mingled sorrow and joy, of grief in the recollection of the past and of gladness in the knowledge of divine and victorious love, "This is a faithful saying, and worthy of all acceptation, that Christ Jesus came into the world to save sinners, of whom I am chief," (1 Tim. i. 15). He no longer affirms, as he once asserted that, touching the righteousness which is of the law, he was blameless, (Phil. iii. 6); but he describes himself as the chief of sinners; and still this most contrite and humble of men assigns to his written word all the authority and power that belong to the acknowledged word of God.

Addressing the Corinthians he says, "My speech and my preaching was not with enticing words of man's wisdom, but in demonstration of the Spirit and of power: that your faith should not stand in the wisdom of men, but in the power of God. . . . Which things also we speak, not in the words which man's wisdom teacheth, but which the Holy Ghost teacheth; . . . for who hath known the mind of the Lord, that he may instruct him? But we have the mind of Christ," (1 Cor. ii. 4-16); "If I come again, I will not spare; since ye seek a proof of Christ speaking in me, which to you-ward is not weak, but is mighty in you," (2 Cor. xiii. 2, 3). So to the Thessalonians he says, "For this cause also thank we God without ceasing, because, when ye received the word of God, which ye heard of us," ye received it not as the word of men, but, as it is in truth, the word of God, which effectually worketh also in you that believe," (1 Thess. ii. 13); "he therefore that despiseth, despiseth not man, but God, who hath also given unto us his Holy Spirit," (1 Thess. iv. 8).

Thus did this meek and lowly man ever exalt his official word to an equality with the word of God, nor did he shrink from standing on a level of authority with Him of whom he wrote, "The love of Christ constraineth us; because we thus judge, that if one died for all, then were all dead: and that he died for all, that they which live should not henceforth live unto themselves, but unto him which died for them, and rose again," (2 Cor. v. 14, 15). This is the man of unswerving devotion to Jesus, who wrote, "Unto the married I command, yet not I, but the Lord, Let not the wife depart from her husband." The Lord Himself had given such a command, when He was upon the earth, (Matt. xix. 6-9). "But to the rest speak I, not the Lord: If any brother hath a wife that believeth not, and she be pleased to dwell with him, let him not put her away." The Lord had said nothing about the question here raised; but Paul gave the command, to which unquestioning obedience was due, just as much as if it had proceeded from the mouth of Christ Himself. "As God hath distributed to every man, as the Lord hath called every one, so let him walk. And so I ordain in all the churches," (1 Cor. vii. 10-17). Is it possible that one who spoke of himself as "less than the least of all saints," as "the least of the apostles," as "the chief of sinners," could establish ordinances for the observance of all the churches, and rise to the height of authority which he ascribed to his divine Redeemer, unless he believed at least that he was infallibly inspired to teach and to command?

But the testimony of the apostle Peter leaves no room for doubt concerning the exact place to which his writings are to be assigned. "Account that the long-suffering of our Lord is salvation; even as our beloved brother Paul also, according to the wisdom given unto him, hath written unto you; as also in all his epistles, speaking in them of these things; in which are some things hard to be understood, which they that are unlearned and unstable wrest, as they do also the other scriptures, to their own destruction," (2 Pet. iii. 15, 16). This valuable testimony is conclusive upon two points: first, that *all* of Paul's epistles were at the time it was given well known to the churches scattered throughout the Roman empire; and, second, that they were to be exalted to the same rank held by *the other scriptures,* of which Peter says, "the prophecy came not in old time by the will of man: but holy men of God spake as they were moved by the Holy Ghost." In like manner Peter speaks of himself, saying, "This second epistle, beloved, I now write unto you; in both which I stir up your pure minds by way of remembrance: that ye may be mindful of the words which were spoken before by the holy prophets, and of the commandment of us the apostles of our

Lord and Saviour," (2 Pet. iii. 1, 2); thus raising his own written word, and the word of the other apostles, to a level with the authority of the holy prophets, through whose mouth God proclaimed His commands to men.

It only remains to notice the manner in which Jesus Christ, and those who claimed to be the inspired teachers of His gospel and founders of His religion, treated the very letter of the scriptures, that were then regarded as the sacred writings of the Jews. The former, it is said, at the commencement of His public ministry, was led up of the Spirit into the wilderness, to be tempted of the devil. Each temptation He met with the simple but sublime answer, "It is written;" and it is a remarkable fact that the scriptures He cites against the suggestions of Satan are all taken from the book of Deuteronomy, so generally neglected now even by Christians. In His public discourses and private conversations with His disciples, He constantly quoted the scriptures, so that "the Jews marvelled, saying. How knoweth this man letters, having never learned?" and the officers who were sent to arrest Him returned to the chief priests and Pharisees with the exclamation, "Never man spake like this man," (John vii. 15, 46). Frequently His teachings turned upon a single word of the Scriptures; and even amid the agonies of the crucifixion, we find Him calmly surveying the wide and variegated field of ancient prophecy, and, "that the scripture might be fulfilled," crying out, "I thirst," (John xix. 28). After His resurrection also His mind seemed to be full of the scripture, for He joined the two disciples on their way to Emmaus, "and beginning at Moses, and all the prophets, he expounded unto them in all the scriptures the things concerning himself," and on the evening of the same day, appearing to the assembled disciples, "He said unto them, These are the words which I spake unto you while I was yet with you, that all things must be fulfilled which were written in the law of Moses, and in the prophets, and in the Psalms, concerning me," (Luke xxiv. 27, 44).

So Paul, who wrote most of the Epistles, often makes a single word from the Old Testament the starting point of a masterly and weighty argument, showing clearly that he regarded the sacred writings as not inspired merely in general, nor in the thoughts of the ancient prophets, nor in different degrees; but in the minutest particulars of all their language. When to this it is added that he and the other apostles exalted their testimony to a position of authority side by side with the holy men of God, who spake as they were moved by the Holy Ghost, some conception may be formed of the claims of the entire Bible to verbal and complete inspiration, and of the perfect unity that pervades all its parts.

This unity is one of the most marvellous things about the marvellous book. Whatever maybe the alleged discrepancies and inaccuracies with regard to dates, numbers, and the minor details of narratives given by its different writers, the most careless reader can not fail to see that all have one general aim and object, and that there is a wonderful harmony in their doctrinal statements. When we consider that there are about fifty human authors of every time of life from early manhood to old age; of every degree of mental cultivation from illiteracy to all the learning of that period; of every rank from the hut of a fisherman to the palace of a king; of every condition, from the depth of mortal sorrow to the height of earthly felicity—when we consider that the first and the last of these were separated from each other by the interval of at least fifteen hundred years—when we consider that they treated every conceivable subject, visible and invisible, in heaven, in earth, and in hell, the creation of the world, the personality and character of God, providence, history, biography, customs, manners, opinions, travels, all the relations men hold to each other and the duties that spring out of these various relations—the remarkable unity that binds their testimony into one magnificent and overwhelming demonstration of divine truth may well excite the gratitude of the Christian mind, and the astonishment of the skeptical mind.

The same mighty Creator, "infinite, eternal, and unchangeable in His being, wisdom, power, holiness, justice, goodness, and truth," is found everywhere. The same story is told throughout of man's sinfulness, and wretchedness, and need; and from Genesis to Revelation the same central doctrine is taught that "without shedding of blood is no remission." It is a book that subordinates every thing to the idea of God, of whose attributes it speaks with a grandeur of conception and beauty of imagery, which renders cold and tame all the allusions to the Deity made by heathen poets and philosophers. It is a book that utters from first to last a stern and persistent and indignant protest against idolatry and polytheism; and that too in the face of man's inveterate proneness to both, as shown by its own records. It is a book that teaches a code of morals which the natural man scouts as altogether unnatural, or denounces as mean and servile, when it attaches to unexpressed lust and unuttered hatred the crimes of adultery and murder, and enjoins meek submission to insults and injuries. It is a book written by Jews, and preserved and venerated by Jews; and yet that portion of it which they recognize is but the monument of Jewish infamy and shame, in the tremendous charges it brings against them of disobedience, ingratitude, unbelief, and worse than beastly insensibility to the claims of Jehovah, and to their own temporal and eternal interests. It is a book that presents to us the portrait of Jesus of Nazareth, which was surely not the product of Greek, or Roman, or Jewish culture, since no such thought ever entered the mind of any ancient writer known to the world, and no such character could have been conceived, because it was contrary to human experience and observation.

While in all these and many other respects, the Bible is so unique that it fully substantiates the proposition, "it is not such a book as man would have made, if he could; or could have made, if he would," it is still more unique, as already stated, in the perfect agreement of its testimony upon every point of doctrine or duty which it presents. Strauss begins his Life of Jesus by reviewing and setting aside as practically worthless those who had preceded him in their attacks upon the credibility of the Gospel history; but where among the fifty writers of the Bible, do you find one who is in conflict with the others touching any leading truth? It can be easily shown that there is not the slightest inaccuracy of statement, or smallest discrepancy of fact, in their entire productions; yet if it be admitted that they are not always harmonious in the trifling incidents of their narratives, how obvious it is that in their great and important thoughts and It is true that each writer has his own peculiar modes of expression, as we can readily distinguish the style of Isaiah from that of Jeremiah, or the style of Paul from that of John; and that this has been urged as an objection to a verbal or plenary inspiration. But the objection may be met by the simple question, who knows the style of God in the plenitude of His power and wisdom? Not only is it asserted by the writers of the Old Testament that He spoke in innumerable instances to the patriarchs and prophets; but the writers of the New Testament mention at least three occasions when He burst heaven open to speak in articulate utterance concerning His well beloved Son. God therefore can speak, and why can He not speak in the manifold style of those whose tongues and pens He employed to proclaim His words? Sometimes a master hand, by the skillful use of the keys and stops of an organ, can make us hear the moan of the storm, the roar of thunder, the murmur of the surf, the singing of birds; and yet one mind suggests and controls and emits these different sounds. Who will say that the Supreme Mind of the universe may not play and act upon the minds and the mouths of His creatures, without the least disturbance of their individual peculiarities!

How else shall we explain the singular preservation from egregious error of these writers who claim, as has been abundantly proved, a verbal inspiration! If the very words of their writings, and of *all* their writings, were not given by inspiration of God, it is clear that they uttered a falsehood deliberately and repeatedly. But if this latter supposition is correct, how can we account for the fact that they denounce falsehood and deception in all its forms, and that their writings, if cordially received, at once lift the soul into a higher and nobler life than it has ever known before? If their very words were not inspired, it is obvious that they can be of no practical value to those who are longing and struggling to reach this higher and nobler life; for not only are we accustomed to think in words, and find it impossible to separate words from thoughts, but in the convictions of conscience and yearnings of heart experienced by every awakened sinner, it is of necessity that the mind stay itself upon something more definite and tangible, and stable, than vague and unattainable thoughts. If the thoughts only, and not the words, are inspired, if the thoughts soar to heaven on the wings of omniscience, but the words are dragged down to earth by human frailty, every one must perceive at a glance that we are drifting in an uncertain voyage upon a dark sea; for in the nature of the case nothing but words can form the guide and rule of our conduct; and if only part of the words are inspired, there is evidently no criterion to distinguish the true from the false, except the decisions of our own fallible judgment. One man rejects one part of the Scriptures because it does not commend itself to his acceptance, and another man rejects another portion, until we shall soon have no Bible at all. Hence Strauss properly characterizes Neander's feeble reply to his Life of Jesus as "an irresolute resistance, like that of a garrison half inclined to capitulate, and already under partial promise to surrender." With a single sentence the infidel assailant forever silences the Christian defender when he says, "He treats the Evangelists generally as writing under inspiration, but an inspiration apart from their educational development as men, and regulating, not the historical, but only the religious part of their accounts: *as if the historical and the religious were not indissolubly connected*," (p. 37).

But, admitting for a moment the correctness of the theory that the four Gospels were not written by their reputed authors, no one will deny that they were written at an age of the world, when the most familiar facts brought to light by modern science were wholly unknown. Errors and mistakes confessedly abound in the works of the greatest authors of antiquity, and in the sacred books of the heathen religions, as those cherished by the Hindoos and Chinese, because they were ignorant of many scientific discoveries with which a school child in Christian lands is acquainted. Such errors and mistakes abound also in the productions of Christian authors who immediately followed the Apostles. Strauss, in his argument against the authenticity of John's Gospel, attaches very little importance to the testimony of Irenaeus, because he says, "The men of old, who saw John the disciple of the Lord, remember to have heard from him how in those times the Lord taught, and said, Days will come when vines shall grow each with 10,000 shoots, and to every shoot 10,000 branches, and to every branch 10,000 tendrils, and to every tendril 10,000 bunches, and to every bunch 10,000 berries, and every berry shall yield when pressed twenty-five measures (about six puncheons) of wine," (p. 89). But the question is, why is nothing of this kind recorded in the writings of John himself?

Again, Clement, mentioned by Paul as his fellow laborer in the Epistle to the Philippians, has left an authentic letter in which he illustrates, or endeavors to prove from analogy, the doctrine of the resurrection. He declares that there is in Spain a bird called the phoenix, which attains the age of six hundred years, and when it finds death approaching, it sets fire to its own nest, leaving only the ashes out of which another bird emerges, and thus it is perpetuated. The same illustration or argument is used by several of the early Christian writers, and similar absurdities and blunders exist in the works of all of them, even of the eloquent Lactantius and the profound and devout Augustine. Why did not Paul say something like this in his sublime discussion of the doctrine of the resurrection?

For the most part the sacred writers were uneducated men of the lowest social rank, totally unacquainted with the schools of learning and the works of philosophers, poets, and orators. They touch upon all topics that affect man's interests in this world or the world to come. Their statements have been subject for nearly eighteen centuries to the severest scrutiny and fiercest criticism; and yet the Christian may calmly and confidently challenge modern science to point to one line or word that is in conflict with known facts. If they speak of the form of the earth, even as far back as the days of Isaiah, 700 years before Christ, or of Job, 1500 years before Christ, they describe it as a globe, (Isa. xl. 22; Job xxvi. 10). If they refer to its position in space, they inform us that it hangs upon nothing, (Job xxvi. 7); and never once do they fall into the error of the Koran, which regards the mountains as created "to prevent the earth from moving, as if with anchors and cables;" never once do they indulge in the folly and puerility of the Shaster. If Jesus alludes to His second coming in the air when His saints shall be caught up in clouds to meet Him, He anticipates the discoveries of modern astronomy, and describes His advent as occurring when it will be night at one part of the earth, early morning at another, and a more advanced hour of the day at another, (Luke xvii. 34-36); and these are but illustrations of the singular accuracy that distinguishes the writings of the Bible from the books of all other religions. Can we fairly and reasonably account for it on any ground except that of divine and plenary inspiration?

Lastly, let us think for a moment of the power and immortality of these writings. Carlyle commences his essay upon Diderot with the remark, "The *Acts* of the *Christian Apostles*, on which, as we may say, the world has now for eighteen centuries had its foundation, are written in so small a compass, that they can be read in one little hour. The *Acts* of the *French philosophes*, the importance of which is already exhausting itself, he recorded in whole acres of typography, and would furnish reading for a life time." Yet, he might have added, who reads them? Only a few years ago the world was ringing with the noise made by the appearance of Renan's Life of Jesus, and the printing presses were pushed to meet the popular demand for a book, which, its admirers claimed, would overthrow the fabric of Christianity. Who prints the book now, who calls for it, who cares for it! It has passed away like a forgotten romance, while the British and Foreign Bible Society alone has circulated nearly seventy-five million copies of the Scriptures in more than two hundred languages and dialects of our race, and the American Bible Society has sent forth nearly thirty-four million copies, besides the countless copies issued by various publishing houses of Christendom.

The precious book still lives, and the more it is read and studied, the more profound becomes the conviction of those who gaze into its wondrous depths that God is its real author. To such you might as well say that man made the earth, as to say that man made the Bible, for the latter not less distinctly than the former proclaims its divine origin,

"Forever singing as they shine,
The hand that made us is divine."

If you read Strauss carefully, you will receive the impression that he possesses a remarkably clear, logical, and acute mind, and a singular power of critical analysis; but how often will you wish to read his book before you have thoroughly mastered its contents? Once, twice, three times, and then you are done with him, because he can teach you nothing more, and to read it again would be like spending your time in going over the alphabet. Yet you may read the Bible a hundred times, and find something you never discovered before, something new, something fresh, something unutterably sweet at each successive reading. To-night a great multitude which no man can number, of the best, the purest, the most gifted, the most useful of mankind, are hanging over its words with tears of contrition, or with smiles of gladness and of hope. They are walking in the light it throws upon their path that without its radiance would be so dark, they are cheered in their sorrows by its tender assurances, they are guided in their perplexities by its matchless wisdom, and they know that, despite all the attacks of infidelity, they will be sustained on a dying bed by its sweet promises.

Last summer, while tarrying for a few days on the sea coast, my attention was directed to a great rock at some distance from the shore. As the tide came in, or the waves rolled high, it was lost to view; but it was still there, and by and by it lifted its rugged head above the waters, unmoved and unchanged. Again and again have the arguments and objections of infidel science and criticism seemed to rush like angry billows over this blessed book; but after a little while it stood forth as of old in its omnipotent and eternal stability. Men may cavil, or men may rage; "nevertheless the foundation of God standeth sure," (2 Tim. ii. 19). "Thou wilt keep him in perfect peace, whose mind is stayed on thee: because he trusteth in thee. Trust ye in the Lord forever: for in the Lord JEHOVAH is the Rock of ages," (Isa. xxvi. 3, 4).

CHAPTER 2
THE CANON OF THE NEW TESTAMENT

Both the Greek and Latin languages have the word canon, and in both it means *a rod, a reed, a measure, a rule*. It occurs five times in the New Testament, and four times it is rendered *rule*, once it is translated *line*. About the age of Jesus and His Apostles it was in use among heathen writers to denote literary works which were regarded as standards of excellence; and soon it was employed by Christian writers to signify the entire scope of doctrine set forth in the word of God as the rule of life; and finally it was applied to the list of the books that comprise the Sacred Scriptures. Only in this last sense is it to be understood now, and the discussion will be confined to the books of the New Testament; partly because they form the principal point of attack by Strauss and other infidels, and partly because their authenticity and genuineness, if fully established, will perfectly secure the canon of the Old Testament.

It is at least worthy of notice that Strauss begins his assault by referring to the labors "for more than a hundred years" of those who had preceded him in their rejection of the Gospel history, and speaks of the issue of these attempts as "each more unfortunate than the other," (p. 5). Further on he says, "such are the lame issues of Schleiermacher's Life of Jesus," (p. 25); and again, "Hase self-complacently calls his 'Manual,' first published in 1829, an essay towards a really scientific life of Jesus; contrasting with it my own work six years later in date, which he calls critically one-sided, and therefore erroneous, or at least useless," (p. 26). His wounded vanity leads him to retort upon his fellow worker in the cause of infidelity by alluding to "the giddiness incidental to the frail footing afforded by his lucubrations," (p. 27), and by pronouncing his view of Jesus "a hopelessly problematical caprice," (p. 28). "I felt satisfied with none of them," he declares;" all seemed to have in some respect failed," (p. 33). Then he comes forward with his own theory, assuming that all supernaturalism of miracle, of prophecy, of inspiration by the Holy Ghost, must be rigidly excluded from the Gospel history, and asserting that its narratives throughout are to be considered, "not the accounts of eye-witnesses, but only fragmentary notes recorded by men who lived at a distance from the events, and who, though they penned down many authentic notices and speeches, collected also all sorts of legendary traditions, and embellished them in part by inventions of their own," (p. 125).

This is the theory that will pass under review; and first of all we must glance at the structure of the New Testament. We find that it is composed of twenty-seven books or treatises, written, as is alleged, at different times and places, and by eight different authors, named Matthew, Mark, Luke, John, Paul, James, Peter, and Jude. How do we know that these men wrote the books ascribed to them? The question conducts us at once to another. How do we know that Strauss wrote his first Life of Jesus twenty-nine years before the second and larger edition, or that Sir Isaac Newton wrote the Principia, or that Bacon wrote Novum Organum, or that Milton wrote Paradise Lost, or that Caesar, Sallust, Tacitus, Livy, Virgil, Horace, Cicero, Thucydides, Zenophen, Aristotle, Plato, Herodotus, wrote the books attributed to them?

Leaving entirely out of view at present the internal evidence of the authenticity and genuineness of the sacred writings, and commencing with the weakest argument, the reply to both of the foregoing questions is precisely the same. We trace the various books mentioned up to the time when they are said to have been written, and no further. We discover a line of witnesses in unbroken succession affirming that the authors named wrote the books, that no one during their life-time disputed their authorship, that no one since, except it be some stray lunatic, has denied it, and that in many instances at least, as Paradise Lost, and the Principia, and the Novum Organum, and Cicero's Orations, no other person or persons could have written such works.

With this accumulated evidence, only a madman, or one in a more deplorable condition than a madman, if he perversely and willfully shuts his eyes to the truth, would persist in saying that the books were not the productions of their reputed authors; for we are so constituted that we are compelled to accept credible testimony. When witnesses who are thoroughly competent in every respect to form and express an opinion, and are shown by their whole character and conduct to be thoroughly incompetent to utter a falsehood, make a deliberate and repeated assertion touching any question that falls within the domain of their personal observation, any question of history or of geography, of facts that can be reached only by the highest attainments of human knowledge or of events that occur in the daily rounds of ordinary life,— when there is no conceivable motive tempting them to make the assertion unless it is true, and when it can not be disproved after the most careful investigation and searching criticism,—of necessity we receive their word, and place it among the things that are positively known.

Most of the knowledge we possess is due wholly to testimony, for not one of us knows anything whatever of the past up to the period of our own childhood, except by testimony. Not one in ten thousand, nor one in a million, knows anything whatever apart from testimony of the statements that are found in the school books, and are universally accepted as the truth, which come to us through the spoken or written word of travellers and of explorers in the lofty and distant fields of science. Yet if we did not receive such testimony, the world would stand still. If all could be induced to take seriously the position, thoughtlessly assumed by so many when speaking of the Bible, that they will believe nothing that lies beyond the range of their own observation, and nothing that is in conflict with their very brief experience, and nothing that refuses to come down to the level of their low apprehension, and nothing that admits the intervention of God's hand in the affairs of God's world, the courts of justice would be closed, the wheels of commerce would stop their movement, the very foundations of society would be rent as with an earthquake, and men would become more suspicious and ferocious than the wild beasts.

Now in studying the canon of the New Testament, nothing more is asked than that credence to perfectly trustworthy testimony, which would be accorded if it were given upon any other subject; and it may be well to remind you that precisely the same sources of information, from which Strauss drew his weapons for attack, have furnished an armory to Christians for a complete and triumphant defence. Where one Strauss has assailed the faith of the best men and women of eighteen centuries, a hundred believers have promptly sprung forward to meet him, not less acute in intellect, not less accomplished in learning, not less pure, conscientious, disinterested, and useful in their lives; and they have hurled back his arguments upon him with crushing force. Sir Isaac Newton, for example, does not hesitate to say, "I find more sure marks of authenticity in the New Testament than in any profane history whatever." Why not believe his testimony here, as we receive his testimony upon other questions that called forth the investigations of his powerful mind? The learned Gaussen of Switzerland, who is certainly the peer of Strauss in every respect, writes after thirty years of close and constant study, "We can fearlessly maintain that in the whole compass of ancient literature there is not a book to be at all compared to our first canon, [twenty of the twenty-seven books] as to the complete demonstration of its authenticity. History does not present a similar instance of literary evidence. Should any doubt the accuracy of this assertion, let him mention a single book in favor of the authenticity of which a tenth part of the same proof can be produced. 'The testimony to its genuineness,' says Michaelis, 'is infinitely superior, and that in numerous respects, to anything that ancient literature could present to us in favor even of the most abundantly attested books.' "So say thousands of godly men and ripe scholars, who have carefully examined every foot of ground over which Strauss journeyed to find objections to the authenticity and genuineness of the books that compose the New Testament. Even he writes as follows, "Thus much is certain that towards the end of the second century after Christ, the same four Gospels as we still have are found recognized in the Church, and quoted in many ways as the writings of the Apostles and disciples of Apostles whose names they bear, by the three most eminent ecclesiastical teachers—Irenaeus in Gaul, Clement in Alexandria, and Tertullian in Carthage," (Vol. I. p. 56). Again lie writes, "In Justin Martyr we gain firmer ground, inasmuch as the genuineness of his most important writings is exposed to no doubt, and the period at which he flourished as an author was, at all events, that of the reign of Antoninus Pius, 138-161, A. D." Strauss then admits that Justin Martyr declares the Gospels "were composed by the Apostles of Jesus and their companions," (pp. 69, 70). Again he writes, "A number of Gospels, and among them without doubt our Matthew and Luke, were known to the heathen philosopher Celsus, who wrote against the Christians about the middle of the second century, and he used their differences from one another, *e. g.*, in the account of the resurrection, as a proof against the truth of Christianity," (p. 75). Again he writes in referring to a work of Origen, "Basilides, about 125 A. D., seems to have already known and recognized the Gospel of John," (p. 84). Again he writes, "It is well known that of all the Canonical books of the New Testament, the Revelation of John is the one the date of which we can determine most accurately from internal evidence," and afterwards he says, John "wrote the Apocalypse in Asia Minor in the year 68," (pp. 94, 100), though further on, he seems to doubt its authenticity, (pp. 373, 380).

These are remarkable admissions from such a quarter. Formerly it was the fashion of a very coarse and very blasphemous and very ignorant infidelity to deny even the existence of Jesus. Now however all infidels acknowledge His existence and that of His Apostles, and then bend their intellectual energies to what they call a natural and rational explanation of the phenomena of their lives in the history of our race. They also confess, as we have just seen, in the quotations from Strauss, that the four Gospels were known in various portions of the Roman Empire, and attributed by friend and foe to the authorship of the Apostles and their companions, 25 years, or at the most 50 years after the death of the Apostle John. But Strauss does not tell us how these four Gospels, if they were not written by Matthew, Mark, Luke, and John, came to be received as genuine in so short a time by thousands of Christians and Churches scattered over the civilized world.

A little further investigation will account for this singular fact. "The Peshito," says Gaussen, "is of all versions of the New Testament the most ancient, the most celebrated, and the most valued. . . . Michaelis, who, with many other eminent scholars, considers it of the first century, or, at the latest, of the second, pronounces it the best of all known versions in regard to ease of expression, elegance, and fidelity. All who have studied it admire the good sense, the erudition, the independence, and the accuracy of the translators." That this version is very ancient may be proved by the fact that the Aramaean-speaking Christians were the first to receive the gospel, that their churches were very numerous, not only in Syria, but on the banks of the Euphrates and of the Tigris, and through the intervening country, and that "their literature was then in a high state of advancement." It was from this version Hegesippus, the most ancient ecclesiastical historian, quoted, according to Eusebius, who says that he lived under Hadrian, from 117 to 138 A. D.; and consequently "Jerome in his 'List of Ecclesiastical Writers' places him before Justin Martyr, who was born in 103, and died in 167. These facts prove the high antiquity of the Peshito version."

"Various other circumstances furnish additional evidence on the same point. The Syrian Christians, from the earliest period to the present time, have with one accord gone so far as to maintain that the Peshito was the original of the New Testament. . . . What further serves to establish the venerable antiquity of this version is the fact of its being unanimously used by the various sects into which the Syriac Christians are divided—Nestorians, Jacobites, Romanists, all employ it in their respective services. Although, according to Wiseman, there are as many as twelve Syriac versions of the Old Testament, and three of the New, none of these has ever supplanted the Peshito in the services of the Church. It must, therefore, have been adopted universally before the appearance of these various sects."

"This version contains the whole of our canon, with the exception merely of the Apocalypse and the four smaller and later epistles of Jude, Peter, and John." The reason for the omission of these will subsequently appear, but it is certainly a striking and suggestive fact that in this most ancient version, running back very nearly at least to the days of the Apostles, we not only mark the absence of every non-canonical book, and we not only find, with the exceptions just named, all the books of the New Testament as we have them to-day, but the arrangement of the books is the same that exists in all of the best and oldest Greek manuscripts. "First, we have the four Gospels, according to their invariable order, Matthew, Mark, Luke, and John; then the Acts of the Apostles; then the Catholic Epistles; and, lastly, the fourteen epistles of Paul in their usual order, Romans, First and Second Corinthians, Galatians, Ephesians, Philippians, Colossians, First and Second Thessalonians, First and Second Timothy, Titus, Philemon, Hebrews."

We next come to the well known catalogue of Origen, who was born A. D. 185, and was martyred at the age of sixty-eight in 253. This remarkable person who, in the immensity of his labors and his power of endurance, was called "the man of adamant," wrote hundreds of books in commentaries and homilies upon the New Testament; and though the larger part of these no longer exists, his works that are still extant consist of four folio volumes. He travelled everywhere to obtain the most authentic copies of the Scriptures that could be found, and as the result of his careful examination, He gives the canon of the New Testament, precisely as we have it, embracing the whole of its twenty-seven books. It is true he distinguishes the First Epistle of Peter, as uncontroverted, from the Second Epistle, in regard to which some doubted; and he also states respecting the two brief epistles of John that all did not consider them as genuine. In relation to the Epistle to the Hebrews, he remarks that some doubted, not its canonicity, but whether it was a production of the Apostle Paul; and then adds, "if any Church receives it as an epistle of Paul, it ought to be held in honor even on that very account, for it was not on light grounds that the early Church has handed it down as a production of Paul's."

Next follows the catalogue of Eusebius born A. D. 270, the favorite of the Emperor Constantine, and assigned by him to the chief place of honor at his right hand in the famous Council of Nice that assembled in the year 325. Of course he had access to all the libraries of the vast Roman Empire, and there is extant a letter of the Emperor entrusting to his care the task of furnishing copies of the Sacred Scriptures. His splendid literary attainments and facilities will not be questioned by any, whatever may be thought of his vacillating character and unsoundness of faith. In his great history he divides the New Testament into books recognize and books controverted, placing in the first division only "the Scriptures universally, unrestrictedly, and uniformly recognized from the first as Divine by all Churches and all ecclesiastical writers." In this class he ranks, "because," as he says, "all ancient teachers and the ancient churches had uniformly regarded them as divine," twenty-two of the twenty-seven books of the canon of the New Testament, or 7,738 out of 7,959 verses that make up the inspired volume. Of the five brief Epistles not put in this class, the Second of Peter, James, Jude, and the last two of John, he says, "These scriptures which have been controverted, though received by most people, and recognized by most ecclesiastical writers, and publicly read along with other Catholic epistles in most churches, have experienced some opposition, and are less quoted by ancient writers."

Succeeding this important testimony of Eusebius we have eleven distinct catalogues in the same century, nine by distinguished "fathers "as they are called, and two by Councils. First, Cyril, patriarch of Jerusalem twenty-four years after the council of Nice, recognizes the canon as we possess it, except the Apocalypse which had not been restored to the. canonical rank it held for 200 years. Second, Gregory of Nazianzus, surnamed "the Divine" gives our present canon entire with the same exception. Third, Philastrius, Bishop of Brescia, agrees fully with the two former. Fourth, Athanasius, perhaps the greatest Theologian of the age, only twenty-six years younger than Eusebius; followed by Epiphanius, only a few years younger than Athanasius; followed by Jerome, bishop of Rome, thirty-five years younger than Epiphanius; followed by Rufinus, an intimate friend of Jerome; followed by Augustine, bishop of Hippo, besides a father whose writings have been preserved, but not his name, all give us the twenty- seven books of the New Testament precisely as they have been held for fifteen hundred years by all the churches of every denomination in all the earth.

In addition to these we have the deliberate decision and decree of two Councils, that of Laodicea, which assembled in the year 364, and that of Carthage which met in the year 397, both presenting as the true canon of the New Testament all of the books as we now read them day by day. Were not the men who composed the Councils better prepared to determine what had been the voice of the Church than Strauss in the nineteenth century? They were more familiar with the writings of those who had preceded them, and self-interest, if no higher motive, would lead them to be exceedingly cautious in announcing their conclusion concerning the books that were to be received as the genuine productions of the Apostles and their companions. The fact that some doubted and disputed for a long time the canonicity of a few of these books is conclusive evidence of the care that was taken, and is sufficient to satisfy a sincere inquirer after truth, that nothing but the most thorough conviction of their Apostolic origin could have led to their final and unhesitating reception.

A moment's reflection will show how the doubt and dispute arose in relation to the Apocalypse, the epistle to the Hebrews, that of James, the Second of Peter, the last two of John, and that of Jude. With regard to the book of Revelation, nothing can be more fully proved than its universal reception at first; but as the hope of the Lord's Second Coming began to decline in the increasing power and progress of the Church, it began to be denied on account of its miliennarian teachings. With regard to the epistle to the Hebrews, like the Apocalypse no one thought of calling in question for a considerable period its right to a place in the canon; but at length it declined in favor with some, because it was supposed to favor the heresies of the Montanists and Novatians, though like 'the Apocalypse again many of the first men in the Church always maintained its canonicity. With regard to the epistle of James, while the

Eastern Church from the beginning received it as authentic, its inspired author never quitted Jerusalem, and because it was addressed "to the twelve tribes which are scattered abroad," Gentile prejudice was slow to acknowledge its authority, like the inconsiderate zeal of Luther, who once spoke slightingly of its claims to authenticity on the ground of its imaginary conflict with the doctrine of justification by faith. With regard to the four brief epistles, they were written at too late a date to become current previous to the close of the Apostles' labors, and hence required patient investigation before they were admitted to a permanent position in God's most holy word.

But all this will only carry demonstration to a candid mind, both of the profound reverence with which the Scriptures were cherished, and of the extreme caution that was manifested until each book could assert its high demands upon the faith of Christians with divine and incontestable authority. It is not true, therefore, as sometimes ignorantly affirmed, that the canon of the New Testament was settled by a few men, or by the vote of councils, but its determination was simply the result of the same sort of knowledge that leads Germany to receive as authentic Strauss' Life of Jesus, to say nothing of the guidance of the Holy Spirit, and the result of concurrent testimony following from all parts of the widely extended Church and from the hearts of believers. As Le Clerc in his Ecclesiastical History well says, "There was no occasion for a council of grammarians to declare authoritatively which are the genuine works of Cicero or of Virgil. In like manner, the authenticity of the Gospels was established and maintained without any decree of the rulers of the Church. The same remark applies to the Apostolic epistles. They owe all their authority, not to the decision of any ecclesiastical assembly, but to the concurrent testimony of all Christians, and to the tenor of their contents."

If we look a little further we shall see that the canon of the New Testament was largely determined in the days of the Apostles, and that it went forth under their sanction. Even Strauss admits (pp. 65, 66), that the sacred writers quote from each other, and in these quotations, as previously shown, they place each other's writings among the Scriptures which they affirm are given by inspiration of God. Let any one with a good Reference Bible read the Epistles, and he will be surprised, if the study is new to him, at the number of manifest allusions to the words of the Lord Jesus and of the different Apostles, the latter being put on a level of authority with the former, and with the holy men of

God in old time who spake as they were moved by the Holy Ghost. Thus Peter in his last Epistle refers to all the epistles of Paul, and declares that the unlearned and unstable wrest them, as they do also the other scriptures, to their own destruction. So Jude refers to this last Epistle of Peter when he says, "Beloved, remember ye the words which were spoken before of the apostles of our Lord Jesus Christ; how that they told you there should be mockers in the last time, who should walk after their own ungodly lusts." It is obvious, therefore, that the canon of the New Testament passed almost, if not altogether, under the inspection of the Apostles themselves, some of whom lived thirty, forty, fifty, and even sixty years after the crucifixion of our Saviour.

Let us suppose that Strauss, having personally superintended the successive editions of his Life of Jesus during the past forty years, and finding no one to dispute his claim of authorship, goes at last, as indeed he has gone, for judgment before Him whose word he has labored so earnestly to overthrow. Let us suppose that his admirers a hundred years hence, if it please the Lord to tarry so long, and if Strauss should have any admirers then, discover that the authenticity of the book is called in question—would they not be surprised and indignant at the effrontery of skepticism in the face of such evidence? But the proof that he wrote the Life of Jesus falls far short of the evidence both external and internal that Matthew, Mark, Luke, and John wrote the four Gospels, and that Paul, James, Peter, and Jude wrote the Epistles ascribed to them. Not only were the writers spared in the midst of incessant dangers for forty, fifty, and one of them for nearly seventy years; not only did they severally and jointly superintend the preservation and dissemination of their writings, and thus guarantee their genuineness; but these writings were in the hands of an innumerable multitude scattered over the world', and hence it was absolutely impossible that they could be changed as Strauss imagines by the addition of "all sorts of legendary traditions and inventions," without instant detection and exposure.

In the first place, we have the undoubted testimony of heathen writers, as Tacitus and Pliny, concerning the amazing spread of Christianity. The former, speaking of the burning of Rome by Nero, and his cruel attempt to fasten the crime upon the followers of Jesus, says, "Those who avowed themselves to be Christians were first taken up, and, afterwards, on their depositions, an immense multitude, convicted, less of having been implicated in burning Rome, than of hating all mankind."

"The most obstinate skepticism," says Gibbon, is compelled to respect the truth of this extraordinary fact, which is further confirmed by the accurate Suetonius, for that historian likewise mentions the punishments inflicted by Nero on the Christians." This was while Paul, and Peter, and John, and other Apostles were still preaching the Gospel. Pliny, an intimate friend of Tacitus, and governor of Bythinia, having received direction from Trajan to punish Christians, writes to his imperial master, "What must I, then, do? The case appears to me very serious, especially on account of the vast number of persons of both sexes, of every rank and age, who are already or will be under persecution. It is not merely in the cities that this superstition has spread, but also in the towns and villages, and even in the rural districts."

Justin Martyr, a little later, reminds the Jew that "there are some countries in which none of his nation ever dwelt; but there is not so much as one nation of men, whether Greek or barbarian, Scythian or Arabian, amongst whom prayers and thanksgivings are not offered up to the Father through the name of Jesus Crucified." Tertullian, only a few years later, writes to the Roman authorities, "We are but of yesterday, and we have filled your empire—all that is yours—towns, islands, fortresses, municipal towns, market-places, the senate, the forum. We have only left you the temples. We can make war upon you without taking arms; it is enough not to live with you; for if the Christians, who compose so great a multitude, should abandon you and retire into some other country, it would be the ruin of your power, and you would be terrified at your own solitude." Again he says, "The Gothic nations, the various Moorish tribes, all the regions of Spain and Gaul, and places in Britain inaccessible to the Romans, have been subjected to Christ, as well as the Sarmatians, Dacians, Germans, Scythians, and nations yet unknown." What a stretch of credulity it must require to believe that all these countless Christians, found over the whole world, permitted all sorts of legendary traditions and forgeries to be added to the sacred books in their hands, and then persisted with unvarying unanimity in asserting that they possessed the very writings of the inspired Apostles! Well might Thiersch say, "We must avow, that incredulity in reference to the first canon, when persisted in, requires the' admission of such incredible and preposterous things, that, in comparison with such gullibility, the blindest belief of some Christians in certain miraculous legends is a mere trifle."

In the second place, no fact in history is better attested than the public reading of the New Testament in these innumerable and widely- scattered assemblies. Such indeed was the direction of the Apostles themselves, as when Paul says to the Thessalonians, in the first Epistle he wrote, "I charge you by the Lord, that this epistle be read unto all the holy brethren," (1 Thess. v. 27), and to the Colossians, "When this epistle is read among you, cause that it be read also in the church of the Laodiceans; and that ye likewise read the epistle from Laodicea," (Col. iv. 16). Accordingly Justin Martyr, in his Apology to the Emperor Antoninus, describing the Christian assemblies, says, "On the day called Sunday, there is a gathering to the same place of all who live either in the towns or country, and then the memoirs of the Apostles, or the writings of the prophets, are read as long as the time allows. Then, when the reader has finished, the president, by an address, makes an exhortation and an appeal to prompt to an imitation of these noble examples." Such was the universal custom, as formed by Jewish Christians in the synagogues, as taught by the positive command of the Apostles, as arising from the nature and necessity of the early gatherings of believers, as kept up by God's people to this day; and surely no sane man will assert that it would have been possible to introduce fictions, and forgeries, and all sorts of traditionary legends, into writings that were publicly read, at least every week, in thousands of different places. Such a thing could not be done now in any country of Christendom, and certainly it could not have been done then in all the countries of the known world, without discovery.

In the third place, not only were copies of the four Gospels and the Epistles found everywhere throughout the Roman empire, but they were so constantly quoted by contemporary and subsequent writers as to justify the remark of Lardner, that were we to collect all the passages of the New Testament cited in the works of Tertullian alone, who wrote in the second century, "their amount would be greater than all the quotations made from Cicero during two thousand years by all writers that are known to exist." Polycarp, for example, a disciple of the Apostles, in a letter whose authenticity is not denied, written only four years after the death of John, quotes extensively and accurately from the Gospels and nearly all the Epistles. Ignatius, who was of John's hearers, does the same thing. Papias, who was also one of John's hearers, directly attributes the Apocalypse to the Apostle. Clement, of Rome, who is mentioned by Paul in his Epistle to the Philippians, wrote a long letter, which has been preserved, and which is full of references to the various books of the New Testament.

The extent to which these quotations were made in the early ages of the Church may be inferred from the following striking fact stated in the Memoirs of Robert Haldane, a Scotch gentleman of wealth and learning, and withal an eminent Christian: "There is an interesting anecdote, which was related by the late Rev. Dr. Walter Buchanan, with reference to the means which seems to have been provided in order to secure the New Testament either from interpolation or corruption: 'I was dining,' said Dr. Buchanan, 'some time ago, with a literary party at old Mr. Abercromby's, of Tulloby, (the father of Sir Ralph Abercromby, who was slain in Egypt), and we spent the evening together. A gentleman present put a question which puzzled the whole company. It was this: Supposing all the New Testaments in the world had been destroyed at the end of the third century, could their contents have been recovered from the writings of the three first centuries? The question was novel to all, and no one even hazarded a guess in answer to the inquiry.'

"About two months after this meeting I received an invitation to breakfast with Lord Hailes next morning. He had been of the party. During breakfast he asked me if I recollected the curious question about the possibility of recovering the contents of the New Testament from the writings of the three first centuries? 'I remember it well, and have thought of it often without being able to form an opinion or conjecture on the subject.' 'Well' said Lord Hailes, What question quite accorded with the turn or taste of my antiquarian mind. On returning home, as I knew I had all the writers of those centuries, I began immediately to collect them, that I might set to work on the arduous task as soon as possible.' Pointing to a table covered with papers, he said, 'There have I been busy for these two months, searching for chapters, half chapters, and sentences of the New Testament, and have marked down what I found, and where I have found it, so that any person may examine and see for himself. I have actually discovered the whole New Testament, except seven or eleven verses (I forget which), which satisfies me that I could discover them also. Now,' said he, 'here was a way in which God concealed, or hid, the treasures of His word, that Julian, the apostate Emperor, and other enemies of Christ who wished to extirpate the Gospel from the world, never would have thought of; and though they had, they never could have effected their destruction!' Again it may be asked, could a book so revered, so loved, so quoted, so guarded, so universally and constantly and publicly read, become corrupt by the addition of forgeries and all sorts of legendary traditions? Impossible.

In the fourth place, the early heathen and heretical writers never thought of denying the authenticity of the books of the New Testament. Celsus, who wrote against Christianity in the first half of the second century, or less than fifty years after the death of John, boasted that he would bring all his arguments from the Scriptures, and not only quoted plentifully from the four Gospels, but from the Epistles. If these Gospels had been formed from time to time by all sorts of legendary traditions and inventions of various and unknown writers, would not the keen intellect of Celsus have instantly discovered it? Would not the calmer and more philosophic Porphyry, who wrote in the next century against the Christians, have known it? Would not the bitter and vindictive Julian, who wrote in the succeeding century, have taunted the Christians with the worthlessness of their records? But on the other hand, they bear witness to the genuineness of the Gospel history by never questioning the authorship of its books. In like manner the various heretical sects, that soon appeared to the number of more than thirty, led on by Marcion, Tatian, Valentine, Heracleon, Basilides, and others, are unanimous in certifying to the existence of the canon as we have it, and to its divine authority in the churches. They might object to this and that book on account of teachings that were in conflict with their own views, but they did not pretend to deny that all of the books of the New Testament were written by the men to whom they are ascribed; nor did they dream of the theory which now calls these sacred books "myths."

In the fifth place, the style of the canonical books can be distinguished in an instant by its solemnity and sublimity and heavenly influence and commanding authority, from all that is spurious and legendary. In the earlier part of the present century, William Hone brought out, in London, a cheap edition of The Apocryphal Gospels, which was afterwards reprinted in this country. He was known as "the arch-blasphemer." For thirty years he was an Atheist, "as," he declares, "I believe every consistent reasoner must be, who rejects Christianity." He attained great popularity as a writer, and acquired immense influence by his advocacy of radical reform. At length he was prosecuted by the government for blasphemy, but he conducted his own defense for three days before Lord Ellenborough, in the presence of vast crowds; and such was his consummate ability that, despite the earnest efforts of the crown, he was acquitted amid the applause of the people. "When I found," he remarked to a friend, "what an outcry there was against me on account of the Apocryphal Gospels, I set to work to read the canonical Gospels, and, oh! what a flood of light burst in upon me! And thus I became a convert to Christianity from conviction." From that time until he fell asleep in Jesus, at an advanced, age, his faith and hope and love never forsook him, and the following verses, written on the fly-leaf of his precious Bible, contain his confession:

"The proudest heart that ever beat,
   Hath been subdued in me;
The wildest will that ever rose
To scorn Thy word, or aid Thy foes,
   Is quelled, my God, by Thee.
Thy will, and not my will be done;
   My heart be ever Thine!
Confessing Thee, the mighty 'Word,'
I hail Thee, Christ, ray God, my Lord,
   And make Thy name my sign."

In the sixth place, the language of the New Testament, and its constant and minute references to persons, places, customs, and historical facts, still further establishes its authenticity. Its language is Hebraic-Greek, or Greek intermixed with Hebraic peculiarities and idioms, such as was spoken in Palestine. It is not the pure and elegant Greek of the classic writers, but precisely the language we would expect from those who are the reputed authors of the book. "We may go still further, and assert not only that the language of the Greek Testament *accords* with the situation of the persons to whom it is ascribed, but that it *could not* have been used by any person or persons who were in a different situation from that of the Apostles and evangelists. It was necessary to have lived in the first century, and to have been educated in Judea, or in Galilee, or in some adjacent country, to be enabled to write such a compound language as that of the Greek Testament." So we find the writers referring, without the slightest hesitancy, and in the most undisguised manner, to various localities, and historical events, and prominent individuals, as Augustus, Herod, Agrippa, Pilate, Festus, Felix, Cornelius, Julius, a centurion of Augustus' band; yet with the single exception of the statement about the taxing of the Jews under

Cyrenius, so far as now remembered, the perfect accuracy of their testimony is not even questioned. Indeed, many books have been written, by Paley and others, setting forth the "undesigned coincidences "that have been gathered by comparing the sacred writers with each other, and that leave upon an unprejudiced mind no shadow of doubt concerning their honesty and strict truthfulness, even in the minutest particulars. Is this the custom of men who are guilty of forgery, and are offering to the world a narrative of pretended facts that are only inventions of their own'? Yet the distinct charge of Strauss is, that the four Gospels are "not the accounts of eye-witnesses, but only fragmentary notes recorded by men who lived at a distance from the events, and who, though they penned down many authentic notices and speeches, collected also all sorts of legendary traditions, and embellished them in part by inventions of their own." It is far easier to believe the most stupendous miracle recorded in the Bible than such nonsense as that.

Let us suppose that a book is published the present year, purporting to contain the speeches and acts of Congress that met one hundred years ago, while it is made up of all sorts of legendary traditions and inventions of the writer or writers. What would be the probability of its success? None whatever. The judges, and lawyers, and politicians, and learned men, would instantly say, it was never heard of before, and they would dismiss it with merited contempt. But this is only a feeble illustration of the impossible thing which Strauss asks us to believe without the slightest evidence. We have already seen that twenty-two of the books of the New Testament, just as we have them, were widely disseminated and read during the life-time of the Apostles, and extensively quoted by various writers immediately after the death of John. Yet according to the theory of Strauss, we must suppose that men, who lived at a distance from the events narrated, succeeded so easily and so universally in imposing all sorts of legendary traditions and inventions of their own upon all the Christians, that their forgeries were not even perceived. We must suppose that, notwithstanding the intense love exhibited by the early disciples for their sacred writings, notwithstanding the watchful jealousy that led some of them to hold in abeyance a few of the minor books of the New Testament until their authenticity was established by the most conclusive evidence, so immediately and completely did these spurious productions sweep away all that had been previously accepted and revered as genuine, that no question was ever raised concerning them by friend or foe. Finally we must suppose that the forgery was so perfect, it has never been detected by the keenest criticism of eighteen hundred years, a criticism far more searching and unsparing than was ever bestowed upon any book, or all the books of the world. He who can believe this can believe the most astounding miracle, not only without testimony, but in the face of all testimony.

In the seventh place, if the Gospel narratives were written by persons who lived at a distance from the events, who collected all sorts of legendary traditions, and embellished them in part by inventions of their own, the history of the world during the past fifteen centuries is founded on a lie, for the history of the Church is the history of the world. All the mighty stimulus to the intellect confessedly found in the New Testament, all of its stirring incentives to enterprise and progress, all of its emancipating power from the bondage of terror, all of its associations with liberty, all of its elevating and hallowed influence upon home and society, all of its attractiveness that has won the admiration of the noblest minds, all of its sweet consolations that have ministered so long and so often to the hearts of the sinful and sorrowing, all of the examples it has furnished of superhuman courage, and unselfish devotion, and of willing sacrifice for the good of our race, and of sustained holiness amid temptations and trials, all of the joy it has brought to the dying, as the name of Jesus has caused the pallid lip to smile, and the dim eye to kindle, all, all is a delusion, or the triumph of forgery! Surely the skeptic who is so fond of exalting the laws of nature that he attempts to dethrone nature's Law-giver, must see that if Strauss is correct, the laws of nature that govern the human mind have been constantly violated, under the government of a righteous God, to sustain a monstrous fraud and falsehood.

Only a short time since, Joseph Barker died in the faith of the Gospel, trusting simply in the blood of Christ to wash away his deep and accumulated guilt. For many years he was a leading Deist, lecturing throughout Great Britain and the United States, perfectly familiar with the arguments of Strauss and other infidels, and challenging every minister, whose attention he could engage, to public discussion. On one occasion when he was leaving his house to stand before the people as an ambassador of Satan, his little child followed him to the door and said, "God bless you, Papa." That little voice, he afterwards declared, kept ringing in his heart. "God bless me!" he exclaimed; "God bless me for what? God bless me in what? For hating His Son? In seeking to destroy His word?" Nor could he get rid of that voice until he bowed at the feet of the crucified but risen Jesus, and found pardon and salvation for the chief of sinners.

Dear friends, may the voice of some little child, a voice it may be you will hear no more, reach to-night any who are skeptical, and echo the gentle and entreating voice that still says, "Come unto me, all ye that labor and are heavy laden, and I will give you rest." But whether you heed the voice of Jesus, or turn away from it in unbelief and indifference; whether you accept at last His own word, that all your hatred can not change His pity nor chill His love, or persist in your enmity to One who has never wronged you; whether you permit Him to make you happy here and hereafter, or choose to go your own way into a dark eternity, let His unworthy servant say in all sincerity and affliction, "God bless you, God bless you."

CHAPTER 3
THE CHARACTER OF JESUS

With regard to the present discussion, it is of no consequence whether the four Gospels were composed by the authors to whom they are ascribed, or by persons of whom the world has never heard. Nor is it of importance to inquire whether the history is "true and reliable as a whole, and in its details," or whether its writers "collected all sorts of legendary traditions, and embellished them in part by inventions of their own." Whatever conclusion infidels may choose to reach concerning such questions, the undeniable fact still remains that in the Gospels we find the portrait of a character, which is the most marvelous miracle of the ages. If there was a real person whose likeness is here accurately drawn. He Himself is the greatest of miracles; if it is only a fancy sketch at which we are called to look, the genius to paint the picture is a still greater miracle, were it possible; as "the inventor," Rousseau well says, "would be a more astonishing character than the hero."

Strauss begins his "Historical Outline of the Life of Jesus" by referring to the influence of "Judaism," and of "Greco-Roman cultivation;" but it is clear that Jesus is not the fruit or result of either. The former, in the sense in which Strauss understands it, as a mere human culture and development, found its expression and manifested its vitality, at the time Jesus was horn, in the three sects of Pharisees, Sadducees, and Essenes. But according to the biographers of Christ, He was in sharp conflict with the two first through the whole of his brief public ministry, and with the asceticism and mysticism of the last it is obvious at a glance that He had no sympathy whatever. As to Greco-Roman cultivation, Strauss admits "it shows itself in the resemblance of the Greek gods to men," and then adds, "It was precisely because the Divinity did not confront the Greek in the form of a commanding law, that the Greek was compelled to be a law to himself: because he did not, like the Jew, see his whole life ordered for him, step by step, by religious ordinance, he was compelled to seek for a moral rule within his own mind. That this was a difficult problem, that the way to the solution of it led over dangerous ground, we see by the corruption of morals which broke in over the Greek nation after the most brilliant and flourishing age, by the arbitrary manner in which the contemporary Sophists confounded all moral notions," (Vol. I. p. 244).

It is true that Judaism in its sacred books had spoken repeatedly of the coming of a mighty and even a divine Deliverer, from the day the promise was made to the fallen parents of our race, that the seed of the woman should bruise the head of the tempter (Gen. iii. 15). The extraordinary manner of His birth is told, as when it is said, "Behold, a virgin shall conceive, and bear a son, and shall call his name Immanuel," (Isa. vii. 14; Matt. i. 23). The place of His nativity is mentioned, as when it is said, "Thou, Bethlehem Ephratah, though thou be little among the thousands of Judah, yet out of thee shall he come forth unto me that is to be ruler in Israel; whose goings forth have been from of old, from everlasting," (Mic. v. 2; Matt. ii. 6). His remarkable character and career are described in glowing language, as when it is said, "Unto us a child is born, unto us a son is given, and the government shall be upon his shoulders; and his name shall be called Wonderful, Counsellor, The mighty God, The everlasting Father [or rather the Father of the ages to come], The Prince of Peace. Of the increase of his government and peace there shall be no end, u]3on the throne of David, and upon his kingdom, to order it, and to establish it with judgment and with justice, from henceforth even forever," (Isa. ix. 6, 7). To these passages might be added scores of quotations from the ancient writings of the Jews, distinctly predicting both the leading events and the minutest incidents in the life, teachings, works, betrayal, sufferings, death, resurrection, and second coming of the promised Messiah; and Strauss imagines that such predictions suggested to the forgers or inventors of the Gospel history the propriety of having them fulfilled by Jesus of Nazareth. But it will be observed that nowhere in the writings of the Jews do we learn how a virgin is to conceive, and bring forth a son, whose name indicated that He was Immanuel, God manifest in the flesh. The inventors of the New Testament history were left to their own invention to solve the mystery.

It is true that Greco-Roman cultivation ever and anon sounded a faint prelude of the song of incarnation, and told out the longings of many an earnest spirit, as that of Socrates, for the descent of Deity to the earth, when its mythology described the birth of beings half human and half divine. But these beings were invariably associated with stories that were coarse, and low, and sensual, and shameful; for they were represented as the offspring of gods who had become fascinated with the beauty of mortal women. Greco-Roman cultivation, at the very height of its splendid attainments, could not rise to the thought of its divinities as exempt from human vices; for having none other than a human standard by which to form an estimate of the superior intelligences, it necessarily attributed to the unknown gods the weaknesses of men, and then experienced the inevitable reaction in an ever-increasing immorality, that at last swept like a flood over the two proudest empires of antiquity. The revolting sketch which Paul draws in the first chapter of his Epistle to the Romans of the state of Greek and Roman society is presented in still darker colors by heathen and infidel writers. Rousseau, for example, tells us that "the paganism of the ancient world produced, indeed, abominable gods, who on earth would have been shunned or punished as monsters, and who offered, as a picture of supreme happiness, only crimes to commit, and passions to satiate."

How comes it, then, that the inventors of the Gospel history, rude, uneducated, belonging to the lowest class, and living at an age of universal vice and corruption, brought their Deity to earth in a way that has never yet shocked the sensibilities of the purest and most refined! Their statement is that the angel Gabriel said to the virgin, "Fear not, Mary, for thou hast found favour with God. And, behold, thou shalt conceive in thy womb, and bring forth a son, and shalt call his name Jesus [the Lord of Salvation]. He shall be great, and shall be called the Son of the Highest: and the Lord God shall give unto him the throne of his father David: and he shall reign over the house of Jacob forever; and of his kingdom there shall be no end. Then said Mary unto the angel, How shall this be, seeing I know not a man? And the angel answered and said unto her, The Holy Ghost shall come upon thee, and the power of the Highest shall overshadow thee; therefore that holy thing which shall be born of thee shall be called the Son of God," (Luke i. 30-35). This is the whole of the wondrous story, and while it can not cause in the most unsullied soul the slightest shrinking, the most debased dare not tarnish it with a breath of pollution. Nothing could be more delicate, more modest, more entirely elevated above all taint of earth; and the bitterest skeptic, who retains a particle of decency or self-respect will bow before the awful mystery in silence, if not with the homage of veneration. Even Strauss, cold, unfeeling, unsparing in his savage criticism, does not hesitate to say, "The view that Jesus was begotten by the Holy Ghost in the womb of a virgin might indeed, as above explained, be reconciled with the Jewish idea of God, by the exclusion of every sensuous element from the conception," (Vol. II. p. 55).

The same amazing skill and utter separation from all that is gross or grotesque, we at once discover in the brief allusion of the Gospel history to the childhood of Jesus. We are told that "the child grew, and waxed strong in spirit, filled with wisdom; and the grace of God was upon him." When twelve years of age, he is represented as accompanying Joseph and Mary to Jerusalem at the feast of the passover, and on their way home he was missed from the group of their kinsfolk and acquaintance, with whom they supposed he was travelling. Returning to the city, "after three days they found him in the temple, sitting in the midst of the doctors, both hearing them, and asking them questions." There was nothing pert, nothing offensive in His manner, nothing that assumed superiority, nothing that was done for display or effect; and hence the only record is, "all that heard him were astonished at his understanding and answers." His mother reproved Him for the anxiety and sorrow she had felt on account of His absence, and He replied, "How is it that ye sought me? wist ye not that I must be about my Father's business I Mary understood not what He meant, and He went down with her and Joseph, "and came to Nazareth, and was subject unto them: but his mother kept all these sayings in her heart," (Luke ii. 40-51). Such is the reference to His childhood; "and in this respect," says Horace Bushnell, "the early character of Jesus is a picture that stands by its. If. In no other case, that we remember, has it ever entered the mind of a biographer, in drawing a character, to represent it as beginning with a spotless childhood. . . . Commonly a certain pleasure is taken in showing how the many wayward sallies of the boy are, at length, reduced by discipline to the character of wisdom, justice, and public heroism so much admired. Besides, if any writer, of almost any age, will undertake to describe, not merely a spotless, but a superhuman or celestial childhood, not having the reality before him, he must be somewhat more than human himself, if he does not pile together a mass of clumsy exaggerations, and draw and overdraw, till neither heaven nor earth can find any veri-similitude in the picture," (Nature and the Supernatural, p. 280).

That this is true will be admitted by all who are familiar with the manner in which heathen writers of antiquity treated the childhood of their demigods, or with the description given by Josephus of the childhood of Moses, or with the stories told of the childhood of Jesus in the Apocryphal Gospels, that were undoubtedly written by well-meaning men very near the time of the Apostles. These last state that Mary gave to the wise men from the East one of her Infant's swaddling cloths, which, on their return to their own country, they worshipped, and then cast it into the fire, but it was not consumed; that having washed the swaddling cloths and hung them on a post to dry, a son of the chief priest put one on his head, and being possessed of devils, they left him; that Jesus, kissed by a bride made dumb by sorceries, cured her; that a leprous girl was cured by water in which He was washed; that a young man who had been bewitched, and turned into a mule, was cured by Jesus being put on his back, and was married to the girl healed of leprosy; that He caused a well to spring from a sycamore tree, and Mary washed His coat in it, and balsam grew there from His sweat; that a girl, having received one of His swaddling cloths from the Virgin, she showed it to Satan, who had sucked her blood, and flames and burning coals proceeded from it, and fell upon him; that He made clay birds, and caused them to fly; that He turned His playfellows into kids; that He killed a boy who had broken down His fish pools, and another boy who ran against Him; that, refusing to say His letters, He withered the hand of the school-master who intended to whip Him, and struck him dead; and that He performed, as a child, a vast number of similar miracles, which it would be too tedious and too painful to mention. The question instantly arises, why did not Matthew, Mark, Luke, and John, record such repulsive fables of His childhood, or if they did not write the four Gospels, why did the forgers, who "collected all sorts of legendary traditions, and embellished them in part by inventions of their own," so carefully refrain, against the whole spirit of their age, from one word that could cause the holiest and most cultivated of men to experience even a momentary recoil? There is nothing inappropriate, nothing impossible to a child in their narrative; but the single glimpse they give us of His early days is in striking harmony with His birth, and with His entire character. All is beautiful, all is perfect, all is divine.

"When," as Strauss says, "after these preparatory considerations, we attempt to approach nearer to the Person of Him for whom it was reserved to pronounce the word which was to solve the riddle of the struggling time," (Vol. I. p. 252), and come to consider His public life, whatever view may be taken of that life, it remains before the world a miracle, in comparison with which every other miracle is of little moment. We behold a meek and lowly man coming forth from the obscure and despised village of Nazareth, the reputed son of a carpenter, without education, without a knowledge, so far as the record goes, of a single book composed by any of the masters of human thought who had preceded Him. "And yet this Jesus of Nazareth," as Schaff, a German fully the equal of Strauss in intellect and literary attainments, well says, "without money and arms, conquered more millions than Alexander, Caesar, Mohammed, and Napoleon; without science and learning, he shed more light on things human and divine than all philosophers and scholars combined; without the eloquence of schools, he spoke such words of life as were never spoken before or since, and produced effects which lie beyond the reach of any orator or poet; without writing a single line, he set more pens in motion, and furnished themes for more sermons, orations, discussions, learned volumes, works of art, and sweet songs of praise, than the whole army of great men of ancient and modern times. Born in a manger, and crucified as a malefactor, he now controls the destinies of the civilized world, and rules a spiritual empire which embraces one-third of the inhabitants of the globe," (Person of Christ, p. 49).

Renan says of Him, "Neither directly nor indirectly, did any element of Hellenic culture make its way to Jesus;" and "happily for him, he knew no more of the grotesque scholasticism which was taught at Jerusalem, and which was soon to constitute the Talmud," (Life of Jesus, p. 75). Having received, therefore, none of the advantages of mental training in any school, sect, or party, He began His public career by gathering around Him a few unlettered fishermen. That career continued for only three years, and then abruptly terminated on the cross, while He was still almost a youth, and before the period when other men, as a rule, have wrought achievements that leave the faintest foot-prints on the sands of time. During the brief interval His associates were very often the disreputable, stigmatized as "publicans and sinners," and generally the poor, with the exception of "Joanna, the wife of Chuza, Herod's steward," and Joseph of Arimathea, a rich man of whom it is recorded that he was "a disciple of Jesus, but secretly for fear of the Jews." But He never uttered a word that could tend to make the poor dissatisfied with their condition, or envious of those in a higher rank, as shown by the fact that to this day Red Republicans and Communists, clamoring for a reform that would spare nothing of the past, and contending for what they call the rights of humanity in the forcible uplifting of the masses, and the violent levelling of social distinctions, hate Him as the greatest obstacle in the way of accomplishing their reckless schemes, and of realizing their wilder dreams. He was then neither radical nor conservative, but pursued his mission apart from all the distractions of earthly questions, "like ships in seas, while in, above the world;" like an unsoiled sunbeam passing through a dirty moat surrounding the castle of divine truth.

Thus refusing to become identified with any caste or strife of temporal interest. His was the broadest and most universal life crowded into those three immense years that has ever been known. Other great men are generally bounded by national lines and aims; and indeed it is by the very intensity of their national ambition and devotion they usually attain their greatness. Strauss closes his preface to the Life of Jesus by saying, "I joyfully hailed the work of Renan on its appearance, when my own was nearly completed, as the sign of a generally felt want; on closer acquaintance I accept it respectfully, and though by no means tempted by its example to alter my own plan, I may say that all I wish is to have written a book as suitable for Germany as Renan's is for France." He does not seem to rise in his purpose above a book that will do for Germany what he expects Renan's book to do for France; but Jesus, against whom he hurls his poisoned darts with such relentless ferocity, embraces Germany and France and all the world in His far-reaching love. Frederick the Great was nothing except to Prussia; Wellington was mighty only for Old England; Napoleon bound the glory of France to the chariot of his vaulting ambition; even Washington can not touch the heart of one who believes in the divine right of kings, and the advantages of monarchy; while Jesus addresses men of all climes and races with equal directness and sympathy and power. Shakspeare is perhaps the most cosmopolitan and many-sided of all uninspired writers; and yet there are millions to whom his words would have no significance, because they are too illiterate to feel any admiration for the play of his poetic genius, or too stolid under the pressure of hard toil and wearing anxiety and heavy sorrow to care for the entertainment he furnishes in his wonderful delineations of human character. But mention the race, or the class in society, or the individual in any continent or on any island, to whom the sayings of Jesus, as recorded in the four Gospels, would be inappropriately addressed. They are daily read in Greenland, and Lapland, and China, and India, and Africa, and the capitals of Europe, and. North North American Indians, touching, as if with the finger of God, every conscience, and finding a response in every heart. The king in his palace and the doomed prisoner in his cell, the profound philosopher and the ignorant peasant, the leader of armies and the slave in his fetters, the spirit bright with gladness and the soul sinking beneath a burden of grief, have for eighteen centuries hung over these sayings with personal concern, and derived from them light and strength and solace and victory. And is this the work of unknown men, who "collected all sorts of legendary traditions, and embellished them in part by inventions of their own?"

Advancing in our investigation, we are at once struck with the humility and modesty of His bearing, as described in the Gospel history. According to the record He never manifested the least ostentation, nor striving for effect, nor self-conceit. On the other hand. He instantly impressed every beholder by His unaffected lowliness. He sought not the notice of the rich and powerful; He courted not the applause of the multitude; He yielded not to the threats and rage of those whose enmity was roused by His solemn and searching words. On one occasion when the fickle populace would have crowned Him as their expected Deliverer from the yoke of Roman oppression. He retired from their view; on another occasion when they thought the Kingdom of God would immediately appear. He uttered a parable that indicated His withdrawal into a far country to receive for Himself a Kingdom, which He would win in the face of His rejection by His own citizens; and on still another occasion, when their Hosannas rent the air. He knew they were tuning their voices for the frenzied shout, "Crucify him, Crucify him." So indifferent was He to public opinion that many of His mightiest works, which would have convinced the doubtful, and silenced the cavilling, He straitly commanded should not be made known; and as far as possible, He shunned the gaze of the curious crowd, save when called to walk the open path of obedience to the Father's will. His favorite resorts were the lonely mountain side, the sea-shore, with the melody of its waves, or the houses of the humble f and so quiet, so gentle, so far from display were His movements, He is declared to have fulfilled the Scripture, "He shall not strive, nor cry; neither shall any man hear his voice in the streets. A bruised reed shall he not break, and smoking flax shall he not quench, till he send forth judgment unto victory," (Matt. xii. 19, 20). No skeptic, however eager his search to discover imperfection in the narrative of His life, has ever yet accused Him of vanity; for His own testimony and that of His Apostles are self-evident, "I came down from heaven, not to do mine own will, but the will of him that sent me," (John vi. 38); and "even Christ pleased not himself," (Rom. xv. 3).

But with all this. His assertions concerning His relation to God, and His claim upon the confidence, the love, the worship, and the entire devotedness of every member of our race, are indeed amazing, and altogether unaccountable and monstrous and blasphemous, if He is reduced to any merely human classification. Here it is important to notice the remarkable admission of Strauss when he says, "In the history of his public life, there is, as the analysis contained in the former book has shown, much that must be recognized as historical both in the facts, *and especially in the speeches of Jesus*," (Vol. II. p. 116). Much, then, must be recognized as historical, that is, as truly related, especially in the speeches of Jesus, for the intellect of Strauss is far too keen not to perceive that it will hardly do to trace the speeches scattered throughout the Gospels to all sorts of legendary traditions, and inventions of anonymous writers. With this important admission in view, let us glance at these speeches, beginning with the Sermon on the Mount which excites the admiration of Strauss.

We find Jesus, after pronouncing a blessing on those who had never been blessed before, enlarging the scope and deepening the significance of the law proclaimed to Moses amid the imposing tokens of Jehovah's presence, lifting it up into a higher sphere, and adding to its requirements with the calmness and assurance of the original Law-giver. He then determines with absolute authority the manner of bestowing alms, the question of prayer, and the mode of fasting; forbids anxious thought about the things of this life; lays a positive arrest upon the common habit of harshly judging others; reveals the fatherly character of God; exposes the deceptions of false teachers; declares that they will stand in judgment before Himself to bear the sentence of their irrevocable doom; and closes His discourse by likening those who hear His sayings, and do them, to a wise man who built his house upon a rock, that no storm can shake, nor flood sweep away.

A little later we hear Him announcing that man must follow Him, and let the dead bury their dead, (Matt. viii. 22); that He had power on earth to forgive sins (Matt. ix. 6); that the destiny of the soul for weal or for woe turns upon the confession of His name before men; that the necessary result of His mission to earth must be variance in every household divided concerning His character; that He must be loved more than father or mother, more than son or daughter, or life itself, (Matt. x. 32-39); that all things are delivered unto Him of His Father, so that no man knoweth the Son, but the Father, neither knoweth any man the Father, save the Son, and he to whomsoever the Son will reveal Him (Matt. xi. 27); that a greater than Jonas is here, a greater than Solomon is here, (Matt. xii. 41, 42); that during the period of His rejection by Israel and His bodily absence from the earth. His Kingdom will exist in mystery and concealment, but at the end of the age He will send forth His angels, and sever the wicked from the righteous, (Matt, xiii.); that He can receive without a murmur of disapproval the worship of men as the Son of God, (Matt. xiv. 33); that all the evils which defile the outward man flow from a depraved heart, (Matt. XV. 19); that faith in Himself will gain any victory, (Matt. xv. 28); that His divinity is the rock on which He will build His Church, and the gates of hell shall not prevail against it, (Matt, xvi. 18); that no man can be His disciple unless he is willing to renounce self, and take up the cross, and follow Him unto death and glory, (Matt. xvi. 24-27), that His transfiguration was not to be revealed before His sufferings, which He plainly predicted, (Matt. xvii. 9-23); that a little child is the symbol of true greatness, (Matt, xviii. 1-14); that we may keep all the commandments of God, and yet without supreme devotion to Himself lack that which will secure eternal happiness, (Matt, xix. 16-21); that the Son of Man came not to be ministered unto, but to minister, and to give His life a ransom for many, (Matt. xx. 28); that His murder by the Jews would lead to their downfall as a nation, (Matt. xxi. 33-44); that He is not only David's son, but David's Lord, (Matt. xxii. 42-45); that He would often have gathered the children of Jerusalem together, as a hen gathereth her chickens under her wings from the lowering storm or swooping hawk, but they would not; and as a consequence their house is left unto them desolate, until in the extremity of their woe they shall say. Blessed is he that cometh in the name of the Lord, (Matt, xxiii. 37-39); that there will be sorrows and troubles and wars and rumors of wars during the entire interval between His departure from the earth and His return, when He shall come in His glory, and all the holy angels with Him, and before Him shall be gathered all nations, (Matt. xxiv. xxv.); that His blood is shed for many for the remission of sins, and that hereafter He shall be seen sitting on the right hand of power, and coming in the clouds of heaven, (Matt. xxvi. 28, 64); that according to the testimony of His enemies He foretold His resurrection, (Matt, xxvii. 63); and that all power is given unto Him in heaven and in earth, (Matt, xxviii. 18).

Such is a mere glimpse at some of the speeches in the single Gospel of Matthew, of which Strauss says, "We, as well as Baur, have always considered, and still do consider, the Gospel of Matthew as the most original, and, comparatively speaking, the most trustworthy. As regards the speeches of Jesus in particular, notwithstanding all doubt upon individual points, every one must admit that we have them in the first Gospel, though not unmixed with later additions and modifications, still in a purer form than in any of the others," (Vol. I. p. 152). But what shall be said of the speeches just mentioned, so hastily and imperfectly, in this most trustworthy Gospel? They are found in every chapter, and such are the amazing assertions they contain and the high claims they put forth, the only choice they leave is between a belief in His true and proper divinity, and a belief in the grossness and madness of His blasphemy. Those who hold that He was a good man, and nothing more, are utterly illogical and inconsistent; for they go too far, or do not go far enough. He constantly declared that He was far above man and angels in demanding the faith and obedience of the race, in swaying the scepter of universal empire, in coming at the last day to judge the world; and if these startling declarations are not true, He is only to be scorned as a base impostor, or despised and pitied as a crazed enthusiast. Think of man or angel assuming power to forgive sins; summoning the world to follow him against the tenderest calls of natural affection, and the very instinct of self preservation; bidding the laboring and heavy laden of earth's toiling and sorrowful population come to him for rest; proclaiming his future advent after death to sit in judgment upon countless generations, and to pronounce the sentence of eternity; and how quickly the boundless effrontery and preposterous conceit of such pretension would be scouted! Yet Jesus set up these pretensions, and for eighteen hundred years they have been acknowledged with adoring gratitude by millions of all classes and races, embracing the most intellectual, the most learned, the most holy, of the human family, because it is instantly seen that there is the most perfect agreement between His lofty claim and His lofty character.

The speeches recorded in the Gospel by Matthew are in fullest harmony with those running through the other Gospels, especially that written by John, the authenticity of which Strauss particularly assails, contrary to his friend Renan and other skeptics, and the authenticity of which has been more completely vindicated than ever, since Strauss wrote his Life of Jesus. But, leaving the infidels to settle their dispute among themselves, it is enough to know that the meek and lowly One distinctly affirms that He is Lord also of the Sabbath (Mark ii. 28); that He refuses to accept the testimony of devils to His Messiahship, (Mark iii. 12); that He declared it shall be more tolerable in the day of judgment for Sodom and Gomorrah than for the city rejecting the testimony of His disciples, (Mark vi. 11); that these disciples addressed Him without rebuke as the Christ, (Mark viii. 29); that He promised a reward to any who would give them only a cup of cold water because they belonged to Christ, (Mark ix. 41); and that on His trial, when the high priest asked Him the question, "Art thou the Christ, the Son of the Blessed!" He distinctly replied, "I am," and was condemned to death for the alleged blasphemy, (Mark xiv. 61, 62).

The same testimony is borne by Him and about Him in the Gospel of Luke, from the time in the first chapter when His birth as the Son of God was announced to the Virgin, and John the Baptist was called the prophet of the Highest, going before the face of the Lord to prepare His ways, down to the last chapter, where Jesus twice asserts that all the Old Testament Scriptures were written concerning Himself. The same testimony is given by John, certifying that He was in the beginning, that He was with God, that He was God, that all things were made by Him, that to as many as receive Him in His true character He gives power to become the sons of God, that He is the only begotten Son, (i. 1-18); that He came down from heaven, (iii. 13); that salvation hangs upon belief in Him, as the expression of God's love for the world, (iii. 14-18); that God is a spirit, and must be worshipped in spirit and in truth, (iv. 24); that the Father hath committed all judgment unto the Son in order that all men should honor the Son, even as they honor the Father, (v. 22); that He is the bread of God which Cometh down from heaven, and giveth life to the world, (vi. 33); that the thirsty are invited to come unto Him and drink, (vii. 37); that before Abraham was. He lived as the I AM, the self-existent, eternal, unchangeable One, (viii. 58); that He was the Son of God, worthy of worship, (ix. 35-38); that He and His Father are one, (x. 30); that He is the resurrection and the life, (xi. 25); that if lifted up from the earth. He will draw all men unto Him (xii. 32), that the Father had given all things into His hands, and that He was come from God, and went to God, (xiii. 3); that He is the way, the truth, and the life; that prayer, if acceptable, must be offered in His name; that He sends the Spirit to abide with His people, (xiv.); that His commandments must be kept, (xv. 14); that the office of the Holy Ghost is to glorify Him, (xvi. 14); and that the Father will glorify Him, with His own self, with the glory He had with Him before the world was, (xvii. 5).

Truly all this is wonderful, and apart from the exploded idea of imposture or fanaticism, which is abandoned by all intelligent and respectable infidels, it is obviously inexplicable on any theory that would lower Jesus to the level of men. He was a man, but he was more. He sat weary on Jacob's well, and, therefore, was a man; but He lifted the redeemed soul of the sinful woman into the joy of eternal life, and, therefore, was God. He slept upon a pillow in the ship, and, therefore, was man; but He stilled the raging of the tempest with a word, and, therefore, was God. He wept at the grave of Lazarus, and, therefore, was man -, but He called the dead man from the tomb, and, therefore, was God. Thus it is everywhere throughout the four Gospels, that present Him as the Son of man and Son of God, man and God, bound by the sensitive ties of a personal experience to all the wants and sinless infirmities of humanity, but clothed with the attributes, wearing the titles, and performing the works of God. Strauss says, between God and man there is "a gulf not to be passed," (Vol. I. p. 274), and yet he afterwards says, "While Jesus was forming within himself this cheerful tone of mind, identical with that of God, . . . he had, to speak with the poet, 'adopted the Deity into his will;' hence, for him, that Deity had descended from his throne of the universe, the gulf had been filled up, the dread phenomenon had vanished;' in him men had passed from slavery to freedom," (Vol. I. p. 281). So he says other natures were not purified until they had gone through struggles and violent disruption, the shadowy colors of which exist forever, "and something harsh, severe and gloomy clings to them all their lives: but of this in Jesus no trace is found. Jesus appears as a beautiful nature from the first, which had only to develop itself out of itself," (p. 282). Again, referring to many of the sayings of Jesus, he writes, "these are imperishable words, for in them truths that are every day getting fresh corroboration are enclosed in a form that exactly suits them, and is at the same time universally intelligible," (Vol. I. p. 347). Is it not safe to infer from Strauss's own premises that Jesus crossed the gulf, and became the sorely-needed days-man between God and us, laying His hand familiarly upon both? But the marvel does not cease with these remarkable assertions on His part, and these remarkable admissions on the part of those who would banish Him from the earth; for He is represented in the Gospels as affirming not only His spotless innocence, but His absolute holiness. It is surprising to read the comment of so fine a mind as that possessed by Strauss upon the words of our Lord to the rich young ruler, "Why callest thou me good! There is none good, but one, that is, God," (Mark x. 18). It is easy to see that our Saviour was meeting the inquirer on his own ground, and answering him from the stand-point the latter had taken, when he looked upon Christ as nothing more than man. If this were true, he had no right to call Jesus good, for none is good, but one, that is God. But everywhere in the New Testament it is declared in the most unequivocal manner, that Jesus was altogether good, that the devil utterly failed to move Him a hair's breadth from His unswerving integrity, (Matt, iv); that He did all things well (Mark vii. 37); that He always did those things that pleased His Father, and no one could convict Him of sin, (John viii. 29, 46); that the prince of this world came at the close of His ministry, and had nothing in Him, (John xiv. 30); that He was made to be sin for us, who knew no sin, (2 Cor. v. 21); that He was holy, harmless, undefiled, separate from sinners, (Heb. vii. 26); that He did no sin, neither was guile found in His mouth, (1 Pet. ii. 22). He never manifested the least anxiety about the salvation of His own soul; never expressed a word of regret for anything He had done or said, or left undone and unsaid; never shed a tear of repentance; never asked for pardon; never breathed a prayer that inspired a thought of confession, or a sense of moral weakness, but with His dying breath actually *commended* His spirit to the Father; and by this alone He is raised above the life of all other men, even the noblest and the holiest. When, therefore, He said to the young ruler, "None is good, but one, and that is God," He was bearing the clearest and most striking testimony to the fact of His real divinity.

If, however, it is true that the most perfect human character only serves by its shadows and imperfections to exhibit in brighter light the character of Jesus, it is equally true that He surpasses all others in the matchless harmony of His graces and excellences. There is not a man or woman living, nor has one ever lived, with a single illustrious exception, however noted for the possession of some striking virtue, that has not had some accompanying defect as a dark back-ground to the lovely picture. Even the most distinguished saints of the Bible had their faults, and marred the record of their lives by failures. Abraham, the most faithful man, uttered a falsehood, at the risk of his wife's dishonor, to shield himself from imaginary danger. Moses, the meekest man on earth, at last gave way to a burst of passion that excluded him from the promised land. Job, the most patient man, opened his mouth and cursed his day, and floundered in the mire of an attempted self-vindication, until the Almighty silenced him by a voice out of the whirlwind. Elijah, the bravest man, fled in terror from the threat of a furious woman, and wished for himself that he might die. David, so honored by the Lord, committed crimes that have left a deep stain upon his memory, and often caused the enemies of God to blaspheme. Jeremiah, sanctified from his infancy, hoped that the man who communicated the tidings of his birth to his father might be as Sodom and Gomorrah. Daniel confessed his sins, as well as the sins of the people. Peter not only denied his Lord, but afterwards dissembled, and was justly withstood to the face. Paul declared himself a Pharisee to escape from the Jews, and was compelled to retract his angry denunciations of the high priest. Even John would call down fire from heaven to consume the Samaritans who insulted his Master.

Why, it must be asked, were no such defects found in that Master's character? Who among men was capable of portraying such a character? An author's productions can never rise above the author's thoughts, as the conception of the statue must be in the sculptor's mind before it can be transferred to marble, and the conception of the painter's sketch must be previously formed before it can be placed upon the canvas. But where was the example that could be copied by the uneducated writers of the four Gospels, who "collected all sorts of legendary traditions, and embellished them in part by inventions of their own f How did it occur to them to describe a faultless human being, and how was it possible for them to succeed in the attempt, unless the reality was before them in their simple and artless narratives, and unless their pens were guided by the Spirit of God? That they did succeed is shown by the fact that even the most accomplished skeptics do not undertake to censure any word or act of Jesus, and never indicate any mistake He made in all the circumstances of sharp trial through which He passed. He was truly the antitype of the fine flour used in the meat offering, for there was nothing rough, nothing uneven, nothing salient about Him, simply because there was so perfect a development of all the perfections of His nature. It may be said of Him in a far higher and truer sense than of Shakspeare's hero,

> "His life was gentle, and the elements
> So mixed in him, that nature might stand up
> And say to all the world, *This was a man!*"

The more these perfections are pondered by the devout student of the Bible, the more clearly they are seen, and the more they increase in beauty, until many a time he finds himself exclaiming, with his affections all aglow and with tears in his eyes, "Blessed Jesus, would that I were with Thee!" If any one imagines he can improve upon the sayings or the conduct of Christ in any instance mentioned by the writers of the Gospels, as Bushnell says, "Give us then this one experiment, and see if it does not prove to you a truth that is of some consequence; viz: that you are a man, and that Jesus Christ is—more."

That such a being should work miracles, it may be said, was unavoidable. With Him they were as natural as the performance with us of the most ordinary and familiar acts, and hence there was no effort, no struggling, no mighty convulsion of soul to accomplish the effects. "He spake, and it was done; He commanded, and it stood fast." Moreover, no miracle He wrought was an idle exhibition of power, but each had a great moral end to serve, a most valuable lesson to teach. It is a singular weakness in Strauss that he assumes from beginning to end of his book the impossibility of miracles; for a clearer illustration of "begging the question "can not be furnished in the history of literature. There is a vast amount of ignorance on this subject, which only shows how readily most men accept popular errors as truth, and hew easily they are contented with shallow thinking. It is commonly supposed that a miracle is a direct violation, or at least a violent suspension, of what are called the laws of nature, when in fact it is neither. It is simply a withdrawal for a time from the action of those laws of a person in whom God determines to take a special interest, or through whom He wishes to manifest His glory. An apple, for example, if loosened from the tree, falls to the earth by the law of gravitation, but if a man's hand arrests the fall, it is not less truly a miracle, so far as the laws of nature are concerned, than any recorded in the Bible. A miracle is just the exhibition of God's majestic hand amid the laws of nature for some wise and good purpose. There are thousands of well-attested facts constantly occurring around us, which every one knows can not at all be explained in accordance with the ordinary operation of the laws of nature, and these too are miracles. It is utterly illogical, therefore, to assume with Strauss that miracles are impossible, and especially is it absurd in the light of the demonstration, that, whatever view may be taken of the four Gospels, Jesus Himself is incontestably the most sublime and wonderful of all miracles; and Jesus Himself appealed to miracles in the trustworthy Gospel of Matthew, as the attestation of His divinity: "The blind receive their sight, and the lame walk, the lepers are cleansed, and the deaf hear, the dead are raised up, and [above all, and more important than all] the poor have the gospel preached to them," (Matt. xi. 5).

Prophecy, also, in its narrow signification of predicting future events, was a natural and necessary endowment of such a character. Again it may be affirmed that, whatever view is taken of the authenticity of the four Gospels, they contain prophecies ascribed to Jesus, which are meeting with a precise fulfillment before our own eyes. Let the two following answer as illustrations and proofs of the statement; First, He predicted the varying success of His cause, amid incessant opposition, through the centuries, never once intimating that it would achieve universal triumph before His second personal coming. On the other hand, only one-fourth part of the seed, which is the word of God, will take permanent effect, and even that with different degrees of fruitfulness, the tares and the wheat will grow together until the harvest at the end of the age; the mustard seed, although increasing until it becomes the greatest of trees, furnishes a convenient shelter for the birds, which He represents as types of the Wicked one; and the leaven the woman hides in three measures of meal, as the symbol of the mystery of iniquity already at work, will continue to spread until the state of society in Christendom will be like the moral condition of the world in the days of Noah, before the deluge rolled over its guilty population; like the utter ungodliness that prevailed in the days of Lot, before a fiery storm devastated the proud cities of the plain. He nowhere promises His disciples or their successors exemption from toil and suffering, but plainly warns them that they are to expect contempt and hatred and persecution, that His followers will constitute but a "little flock," and that His Church will be like the vessel driven by contrary winds, and tossed upon the bosom of the tempest, when He came walking on the rolling billows. Did ever the founder of any other religion stimulate his adherents to fidelity by such a picture and prospect as this? Well may we exclaim with David, "And is this the manner of man, O Lord God?" (2 Sam. vii. 19).

Second, when the disciples called the attention of Jesus to the goodly stones of the temple, He announced its speedy overthrow, and the desolation by armies of the city in which it stood, and then added, "They shall fall by the edge of the sword, and shall be led away captive into all nations; and Jerusalem shall be trodden down of the Gentiles, until the times of the Gentiles be fulfilled," (Luke xxi. 24). It is well known that Julian the Apostate determined to rebuild the temple, and thus, by defeating the prophecy, to shatter at one blow the colossal claims of Jesus to divinity. He commanded the Jews from all parts of the widely-extended Roman empire to accomplish the most agreeable task, and, as Gibbon says, "Every purse was opened in liberal contributions, every hand claimed a share in the pious labor; and the commands of a great monarch were executed by the enthusiasm of a whole people. Yet," he adds, "on this occasion, the joint efforts of power and enthusiasm were unsuccessful; and the ground of the Jewish temple, which is now covered by a Mohametan mosque, still continued to exhibit the same edifying spectacle of ruin and desolation. . . . But the Christians entertained a natural and pious expectation, that, in this memorable contest, the honor of religion would be vindicated by some signal miracle. An earthquake, a whirlwind, and a fiery eruption, which overturned and scattered the new foundations of the temple, are attested, with some variations by contemporary and respectable evidence." Then, after referring to Ambrose, bishop of Milan, the eloquent Chrysostom, and Gregory Nazianzen as witnesses, he says, '* The last of these writers has boldly declared, that this preternatural event was not disputed by the infidels; and his assertion, strange as it may seem, is confirmed by the unexceptionable testimony of Ammianus Marcellinus," as follows: "'Whilst Alypius, assisted by the governor of the province, urged, with vigor and diligence, the execution of the work, horrible balls of fire breaking out near the foundations, with frequent and reiterated attacks, rendered the place, from time to time, inaccessible to the scorched and blasted workmen; and the victorious element continuing in this manner obstinately and resolutely bent, as it were, to drive them to a distance, the undertaking was abandoned.' Such authority should satisfy a believing, and must astonish an incredulous, mind," (Decline and Fall of the Roman Empire, Vol. II. pp. 438, 439). However science or skepticism may choose to account for it, the fact is, the temple has never been rebuilt.

It is well known, too, that during the Crusades, Europe was rallied, as a continent has never been roused before nor since, by the battle shout, "Rescue the holy sepulchre from the grasp of the Moslem." Army after army of enthusiastic soldiers, animated by the hope of winning heaven, and led by the bravest and most skillful princes and generals, poured into Palestine, only to be baffled by successive disasters and defeats. Even for the little time they succeeded in planting the banner of the cross upon the walls of the sacred city, Jerusalem was still trodden down of the Gentiles, for the European invaders were no less Gentiles than the followers of Mohamet. It is still trodden down of the Gentiles, so that the miracle of Christ's prophecies, or of the prophecies recorded in the Gospels, concerning the condition of the Church and of Jerusalem through subsequent centuries, is enacted at this day before the face of the whole world.

But why speak of the miracles of His deeds and prophecies, when His mightiest miracle is the reign of His love over those who believe in His name? It is the glory of the Gospel that it reveals to us not merely deliverance, but a Deliverer; not redemption only, but a Redeemer; and there is a vast difference between submitting to ecclesiastical rules, or even accepting a system of theological doctrines, and casting ourselves upon a beating heart. Millions, during these eighteen hundred years, have trusted in Jesus as a living Person, and have learned in a happy experience that His sweet promise of rest was not uttered in vain. The conscience, turned into a blood-hound in the breast, and pursuing the wretched fugitive fleeing in vain from the memory of the past, has found protection and peace in His presence; the form, quivering with grief beside the grave that had swallowed up its treasures, has felt the soothing touch of His comforting band; the mind groping in the gloom of a cheerless skepticism has been raised by His tender call to soar amid scenes of supernal light and beauty; and the soul has left behind it the broken fetters of sin, that it may go forth upon a career of joyful and ennobling consecration to Him who is still saying, "The Son of man is come to seek and to save that which was lost," (Luke xix. 10). Blessed

Lord, eternity will be short to tell out what we owe Thine amazing grace!

Hark! He speaks again: "I am the bread of life: he that cometh to me shall never hunger; and he that believeth on me shall never thirst," (John vi. 35). O hungry and thirsty ones, will ye not heed that entreating and persuasive voice? It is a hunger only He can satisfy, a thirst none but He can quench. Come to Him to-night with all your doubts and fears and questionings, and learn the meaning of the precious invitation that seals the Canon of Scripture, "Whosoever will, let him take the water of life freely," (Rev. xxii. 17). Come to Him as One who has the heart of a brother to sympathize, and the arm of a God mighty to save. Then can you enter into the gladness of those who through the "little while "are waiting and watching for Jesus, and who will so soon shout the harvest song at His glorious coming,

"Bring forth the royal diadem,
And crown Him Lord of all."

CHAPTER 4
HUMAN ESTIMATE OF JESUS

It did not fall within the purpose of Strauss to discuss the authenticity of the epistles found in the New Testament, but he acknowledges the genuineness at least of those attributed to Paul, (Vol. I. pp. 412-420). So far, however, as the present argument is concerned it may be admitted that neither he, nor James, nor Peter, nor John, nor Jude, wrote the letters severally ascribed to them. It may be further admitted, if the skeptic so desires, that these letters are not inspired, but are the productions of certain unknown men, who "collected also all sorts of legendary traditions, and embellished them in part by inventions of their own." Still no one is foolish enough to deny that they were written very near the time of Jesus, or that they express the estimate that was formed at that early day of His person and character and claims.

We open, then, the Epistle to the Romans, which is placed at the beginning of these ancient writings, and we are struck with the first clause of the first verse, which says, "Paul, a servant [literally a slave] of Jesus Christ." In the preceding book, called the Acts of the Apostles, that is so largely occupied with the labors and travels and sufferings of Paul, it is obvious at a glance that he merited the designation of a willing and free slave, for he had but one Master and one object in view, and that was Christ. He journeyed everywhere, exposed to danger in every form, stoned, beaten with rods, imprisoned, shipwrecked, yet unfaltering in his devotion, and always bearing in his hand a banner with this strange device, "God forbid that I should glory, save in the cross of our Lord Jesus Christ, by whom the world is crucified unto me, and I unto the world," (Gal. vi. 14). It is in perfect agreement, therefore, with his previous history to speak of himself as the slave of Jesus Christ.

In the second statement of the Epistle he announces that the gospel of God is "concerning his Son Jesus Christ our Lord, which was made of the seed of David according to the flesh; and declared to be the Son of God with power, according to the Spirit of holiness, by the resurrection from the dead: by whom we have received grace and apostleship, for obedience to the faith among all nations, for his name: among whom are ye also the called of Jesus Christ: to all that be in Rome, beloved of God, called to be saints: Grace to you, and peace from God our Father, and the Lord Jesus Christ. First, I thank my God through Jesus Christ for you all, that your faith is spoken of throughout the whole world, . . . For I am not ashamed of the gospel of Christ: for it is the power of God unto salvation, to every one that believeth; to the Jew first, and also to the Greek." Whatever may be thought of such language by the infidel, surely amazing as exhibiting the estimate put upon the character of Jesus. The gospel is said to be concerning Him; He is called our Lord, and the Son of God; all Christians are chosen by Him; He is addressed in terms of equality with God the Father as the object of worship, and the source of grace and peace; thanks are offered through Him; and His gospel is the channel for the communication of God's power unto salvation, (i. 1-8; 16).

In the next chapter Paul alludes to "the day when God shall judge the secrets of men, by Jesus Christ, according to my gospel," ii. 16). In the next chapter, after bringing in all the world, including both Jew and Gentile, guilty before God, he tells us of "the righteousness of God, which is by faith of Jesus Christ, unto all and upon all them that believe; for there is no difference: for all have sinned, and come short of the glory of God; being justified freely by his grace, through the redemption that is in Christ Jesus: whom God hath set forth to be a propitiation through faith in his blood, to declare his righteousness for the remission of sins that are past, through the forbearance of God; to declare, I say, at this time, his righteousness: that he might be just, and the justifier of him which believeth in Jesus," (iii. 22-26).

In the next chapter he refers to the faith that was imputed to Abraham for righteousness, and then adds, "Now it was not written for his sake alone, that it was imputed to him: but for us also, to whom it shall be imputed, if we believe on him that raised up Jesus our Lord from the dead; who was delivered for our offences, and was raised again for our justification," (iv. 23-25). In the next chapter he says, "Therefore being justified by faith, we have peace with God through our Lord Jesus Christ; . . . for when we were yet without strength, in due time Christ died for the ungodly; . . . while we were yet sinners, Christ died for us; . . . if when we were enemies, we were reconciled to God by the death of his Son, much more, being reconciled, we shall be saved by his life. And not only so, but we also joy in God, through our Lord Jesus Christ, by whom we have now received the atonement, [or reconciliation]; . . . that as sin hath reigned unto death, even so might grace reign, through righteousness, unto eternal life, by Jesus Christ our Lord," (v. 1, 6, 8, 10, 11, 21).

In the next chapter he says, "Know ye not, that so many of us as were baptized into Jesus Christ were baptized into his death?... Knowing that Christ, being raised from the dead, dieth no more; . . . likewise reckon ye also yourselves to be dead indeed unto sin, but alive unto God through Jesus Christ our Lord;. ".. for the wages of sin is death; but the gift of God is eternal life, through Jesus Christ our Lord," (vi. 3, 9, 11, 23). In the next chapter he says, "Wherefore, my brethren, ye also are become dead to the law by the body of Christ;" and after describing the writhings of a soul in the grasp of the law, and its fruitless efforts to attain unto holiness by struggling, he exclaims, "I thank God, through Jesus Christ our Lord," (vii. 4, 25). In the next chapter he says, "There is, therefore, now no condemnation to them which are in Christ Jesus; for the law of the Spirit of life in Christ Jesus hath made me free from the law of sin and death; . . . it is Christ that died, yea rather, that is risen again, who is even at the right hand of God, who also maketh intercession for us; who shall separate us from the love of Christ f '(viii. 1, 2, 34, 35). In the next chapter he describes the Israelites, as those "to whom pertaineth the adoption, and the glory, and the covenants, and the giving of the law, and the service of God, and the promises; whose are the fathers, and of whom, as concerning the flesh, Christ came, who is over all, God blessed forever. Amen," (ix. 4, 5). In the next chapter he says, "Christ is the end of the law for righteousness to every one that believeth; . . . if thou shalt confess with thy mouth the Lord Jesus, and shalt believe in thine heart that God. hath raised him from the dead, thou shalt be saved," x. 4, 9). In the next chapter he says, "There shall come out of Sion the Deliverer, and shall turn away ungodliness from Jacob," (xi. 26). In the next chapter he says, "We, being many, are one body in Christ, and every one members one of another," (xii. 5). In the next chapter he says, "Put ye on the Lord Jesus Christ, and make not provision for the flesh, to fulfil the lusts thereof," (xiii. 14). In the next chapter he says, "To this end Christ both died, and rose, and revived, that he might be Lord both of the dead and the living; ... for we shall all stand before the judgment seat of Christ," (xiv. 9, 10). In the next chapter he mentions the name of Christ in twelve verses, closing with the entreaty, "Now I beseech you brethren, for the Lord Jesus Christ's sake, and for the love of the Spirit, that ye strive together with me in your prayers to God for me," (xv. 3, 5, 6, 7, 8, 16, 17, 18, 19, 20, 29, 30). In the last chapter he mentions Christ in seventeen verses, concluding with the doxology, "To God only wise, be glory, through Jesus Christ, for ever. Amen," (xvi. 27).

Now, let it be borne in mind, that if all this is the mistaken opinion of a deluded fanatic or enthusiast, nevertheless it is a human estimate of Jesus, and such an estimate as was never placed upon any other man. From first to last lie is set forth as one with God, as so exalted in His nature and rank it is proper to address to Him our supplications, as over all, God blessed forever, as securing by His death the salvation of the soul, as the only medium through which eternal life is conveyed, as the object of faith, as the Deliverer from sin, as the Head of a new creation coming in after the ruin of the old creation under Adam, as the Judge at whose bar the countless millions of the human race must stand to hear the decision that will fix their eternal state. Truly this is wonderful, and it is the more wonderful, because it is in such marked contrast with the manner in which the writer uniformly describes human nature, as enmity against God, as having in it no good thing; because he exhibits no disposition for hero-worship when he speaks of the most distinguished men, as Abraham and David; and because it is the testimony of one who confesses that he had formerly been a bitter enemy of the crucified Nazarene. In his defence before King Agrippa, he says, "I verily thought with myself, that I ought to do many things contrary to the name of Jesus of Nazareth," (Acts xxvi. 9); but here he wears the title of Jesus' slave, as the badge of highest honor, and the garland of immortality.

The same intense devotion, the same lofty ascription of divine attributes, titles, perfections, works and worship to Jesus, the same constant allusion to Him, as if the soul thrilled with gladness at the mention of His name, pervade all the Epistles of Paul. There is not time for an extended proof of this, which it is needless to present to those who have the least familiarity with his writings; but a glance at the opening chapter of the First Epistle to the Corinthians, immediately following that to the Romans, will furnish an illustration of all the rest: "Paul, called to be an apostle of Jesus Christ through the will of God, and Sosthenes our brother, unto the church of God which is at Corinth, to them that are sanctified in Christ Jesus, called to be saints, with all that in every place call upon the name of Jesus Christ our Lord, both theirs and ours: Grace be unto you, and peace, from God our Father, and from the Lord Jesus Christ. I thank my God always on your behalf, for the grace of God which is given you by Jesus Christ; that in everything ye are enriched by him, in all utterance, and in all knowledge; even as the testimony of Christ was confirmed in you: so that ye come behind in no gift; waiting for the coming of the Lord Jesus Christ: who shall also confirm you unto the end, that ye may be blameless in the day of our Lord Jesus Christ. God is faithful, by whom ye were called unto the fellowship of his Son Jesus Christ our Lord. . . . The Jews require a sign, and the Greeks seek after wisdom: but we preach Christ crucified, unto the Jews a stumbling block, and unto the Greeks foolishness; but unto them which are called, both Jews and Greeks, Christ, the power of God, and the wisdom of God. . . . Of him are ye in Christ Jesus, who of God is made unto us wisdom, and righteousness, and sanctification, and redemption," (1 Cor. i. 1-9, 22-24, 30).

So in the opening chapter of the Epistle to the Hebrews, there are seven assertions concerning Jesus, which show the estimate placed upon Him by His Apostles, or at least by the early Christians. First, it is declared that He made the worlds, that He is the brightness of God's glory, or rather, the effulgence, the outshining of His glory, sustaining to the Father the relation of a sunbeam to the sun, and that He is the express image of God's person, or rather, the exact expression of His substance. Second, it is announced that He upholds all things by the word of His power, that by Himself He purged our sins, and sat down on the right hand of the Majesty on high. Third, at His resurrection God is represented as saying, "Thou art my Son, this day have I begotten thee." Fourth, He is next viewed in His personal relationship to God who says, "I will be to him a Father, and he shall be to me a Son." Fifth, this is followed by a reference to His second coming, when an imperial decree shall go forth from heaven's throne, "Let all the angels of God worship him." Sixth, a glimpse of His millennial reign succeeds, when the Father says to the Son, "Thy throne, O God, is forever and ever: a sceptre of righteousness is the sceptre of thy Kingdom." Seventh, His glory through eternal ages is proclaimed, "Thou, Lord, in the beginning hast laid the foundation of the earth; and the heavens are the works of thine hands: they shall perish, but thou remainest: and they all shall wax old as doth a garment; and as a vesture shalt thou fold them up, and they shall be changed: but thou art the same, and thy years shall not fail," (Heb. i. 1-12).

Was there ever so high an estimate as this placed upon any other being, human or angelic? But thus it is, through the whole of Paul's writings that may be easily read in two or three hours; and yet in these brief writings he speaks of his Master 233 times under the title of *' Jesus," 416 times under the title of "the Christ "or Messiah, and nearly 300 times under the title of "Lord," as implying absolute sovereignty, supreme authority, universal dominion. By one or another of these titles he mentions the crucified One in every chapter of every Epistle, with a single exception, (1 Cor. xiii.); and that exception presents a picture of Him, so exquisite in its coloring, and so lovely in its lineaments, the most careless observer will recognize the excellence of the portrait, without the necessity of reading the name. With Paul Jesus is clearly the motive and the end, the cause and the effect, the centre and the circumference; giving sanction to every exhortation, enforcing every appeal, vitalizing every exhortation, filling every promise with sweetness and with assurance of hope. So completely was his existence absorbed in Him whom he had despised and hated and persecuted, he could truthfully say, "to me to live is Christ," (Phil. i. 21); for without Christ, life would have lost its charm and meaning and power and purpose. But this is not less true of James, and Peter, and John, and Jude, the last of whom although the "brother "of Jesus on the maternal side, calls himself His slave. They also in their short Epistles trace every blessing, every hope, every truth to Him whom they recognize as their Master, and mention Him 41 times under the name of "Jesus," 43 times under the name of "Lord," and 50 times under the name of *' Christ." He was manifestly "all in all" to those who wrote the New Testament.

Of the last book it contains, the Revelation of John, Strauss says, it is "the only writing of our New Testament which perhaps comes from an immediate disciple of Jesus," (Vol. II. p. 437). He admits, therefore, the authenticity of this last book, and yet the estimate put upon Jesus here is higher, if it were possible, than in any preceding book. It opens with a doxology "unto him that loved us, and washed us from our sins in his own blood, and hath made us kings and priests unto God and his Father;" it represents Him as saying, "I am the first and the last: I am the living One who became dead; and behold, I am living unto the ages of ages, and have the keys of death and of hell," (Rev. i. 5, 6, 17, 18); it exhibits Him as sending solemn and searching messages to the Church in its successive development and various phases, until in its last worldly and apostate form it shall be spued out of His mouth, (ii., iii.); it shows us the whole vast assemblage of saints in heaven, singing a new song, and bowing before the throne of Jesus with the rapturous and everlasting ascription of praise, "Thou wast slain, and hast redeemed us to God by thy blood, out of every kindred, and tongue, and people, and nation," (v. 9); it describes Him as presiding over the judgments that shall smite the earth with the thunder-strokes of God's wrath, when the true believers of the present dispensation shall have been caught up above the terrible storm, (vi.-xviii.); it pictures His second appearing with eyes as a flame of fire, and many crowns on His head, and on His vesture and on His thigh a name written. KING OF KINGS, AND LORD OF LORDS, (xix. 12-16); it closes with the prayer, "The grace of our Lord Jesus Christ be with you all. Amen," (Rev. xxii. 21).

Whatever treatment, therefore, the New Testament may receive at the hands of skeptical critics, none will deny that it everywhere gives to Jesus "a name which is above every name: that at the name of Jesus every knee should bow, of those in heaven, and those in earth, and those under the earth; and that every tongue should confess that Jesus Christ is Lord, to the glory of God the Father," (Phil. ii. 9-11). In the four Gospels, the Acts of the Apostles, the twenty-one Epistles, and the Apocalypse, He appears so prominently on every page. He is so completely the sum and substance of all doctrinal teachings and practical precepts. He is so entirely the warp and the woof of the wondrous fabric, that to tear His name away, or to lower Him to the level of ordinary humanity, would leave us only a few worthless shreds, waiting to be swept into the gutter. Take away the name of Jesus, or deny that He was supernatural, and what will you make of the immense and imposing system of Christianity, that did so much even for the intellect of Strauss although he was doubtless unconscious of it, and that has accomplished so much directly and indirectly for the human race? You will then have a magnificent edifice without a foundation, a stream imparting a fertility and beauty which all can see, and yet without a source. Will you account for the estimate placed upon Jesus by the writers of the New Testament on the theory that they were impostors? "The hypothesis of imposture," says Schaff "is so revolting to moral as well as common sense, that its mere statement is its condemnation. It has never been seriously carried out, and no scholar of any decency and self-respect would now dare to profess it openly," (Person of Christ, p. 136). Neither Banr, Strauss, Renan, nor any other skeptic, who possessed sufficient intelligence to render him worthy of the slightest notice, assumes that the men who left us this wonderful book were wilful deceivers and hypocrites; for the assertion would carry with it a thorough refutation in the light of the fact, that they sacrificed home and country and kindred and life itself for what they must have known was a falsehood, that they everywhere threaten falsehood with the vengeance of eternal damnation, and that such a supposition would commit the God of the universe to the approval of fraud and forgery, as the chosen means of communicating the richest blessings He has ever bestowed upon the world. Do you say that they were fanatics? Still the question remains, why did they bow at the feet of Jesus as the only man whom they agreed to exalt above man; and how did the writings of a few ignorant fanatics become so entrenched in the citadel of truth that the discharge of the heaviest artillery upon them has not produced the least perceptible effect in the judgment of the best minds; and what is their charm that, according to the confession of their enemies, they turn every desert in which they are really planted into an oasis, watered with springs, and lovely with verdure!

But following the writers of the New Testament, it may be said that during the succeeding three hundred years there were literally millions of men and women, who placed upon Jesus the same high estimate. For His sake they encountered untold agonies, exile, imprisonment, the expostulations and tears and curses of their friends, the rack, the faggot, the headsman's axe, the wild beast; and when death had done its worst, the inscriptions placed over their bones or ashes witnessed that their faith in a divine Saviour had sustained them in the last shock. These inscriptions are in marked contrast with the gloom which hung over the graves of the heathen, for they are always radiant with peace and joy and hope, as shown in the catacombs. "Asleep in Jesus," "Gone to be with Christ," "Waiting till He come," and similar expressions, indicate that when they lived they lived unto the Lord, and when they died they died unto the Lord, so that death became to them but the portals through which they entered the presence of Him they loved so well, reminding us of the sweet words written on the tomb of Dean Alford, "The inn of a traveller on his way to the New Jerusalem." The force of the argument is not weakened, even if it be conceded that the myriads who endured inconceivable sufferings for the sake of Jesus were silly enthusiasts; for none will deny that they held Him in such esteem. He absorbed every other affection, aroused them to the most intense personal devotion, incited them to deeds of unexampled heroism, and rendered them indifferent to danger. Such esteem added to a purity of life, which even Gibbon. "acknowledges, when he says, "the primitive Christian demonstrated his faith by his virtues," (Vol. I. p. 544), was absolutely essential to the remarkable spread of Christianity in the three first centuries; for nothing but a cordial belief of the testimony borne concerning Jesus by the Apostles and Evangelists could have possibly produced such stupendous results. As late as the year 325 when the Council of Nice assembled, by far the larger part of those who composed that famous Council "had lived," as Stanley tells us, "through the last and worst of the persecutions, and they now came like a regiment out of some frightful siege or battle, decimated and mutilated by the tortures or the hardships they had undergone," (History of the Eastern Church, p. 186). What but an abiding confidence that He in whom they trusted was "over all, God blessed forever," could have kept them true to Him in the midst of their sore trials, when, unlike Mahomet, He had forbidden them to use the sword, when He had held out no hope of earthly reward, and no promise of sensual delight in the paradise beyond?

Passing from these early and innumerable witnesses to the estimate placed upon Jesus by His followers, reference maybe made to the admissions of His enemies. No importance will be attached in the argument to the confession of Pilate, when "he took water, and washed his hands before the multitude, saying, I am innocent of the blood of this just person: see ye to it;" nor to the confession of the Roman Centurion who superintended the crucifixion, "Truly this was the Son of God," (Matt, xxvii. 24, 51); for the skeptic may call in question the truth of the narrative. But he will not question the veracity of his own friends, and their statements are simply amazing as will be shown. Lardner in his "Collection of Ancient Jewish and Heathen Testimonies to the truth of the

Christian Religion," filling four large volumes, quotes about seventy writers of the first six centuries, who used their pens against Christ and His cause. Of these it may be said in general that they often recognize the accuracy of the New Testament writings with regard to persons, places, and historical events; that they do not deny the authenticity of these writings, however earnestly they argue against their credibility; that they frequently at least manifest an exalted estimate of the character of Jesus; and that they usually express their belief in the reality of His miracles. Porphyry, for example, in his Philosophy of Oracles writes, "It will perhaps seem strange to some which we are about to say. For the Gods declared Christ to be most pious, and to be made immortal, and they spoke honorably of Him. When we inquired concerning Christ, whether He be a God, the answer was: That the soul is immortal after the death of the body, knows every body who is favored with wisdom. But the soul of that man is most eminent for piety. Him therefore he declared to be most pious, and his soul, like the souls of others, after death made immortal, which the ignorant Christians worship," (Lardner, Vol. III. p. 209).

The emperor Julian himself, the bitterest of all opposers of Christianity, "allows that Jesus was born in the reign of Augustus, at the time of the taxing made in Judea by Cyrenius: that the Christian religion had its rise, and began to be propagated in the times of the Emperors Tiberius and Claudius. He bears witness to the genuineness and authenticity of the four Gospels of Matthew, Mark, Luke, and John, and the Acts of the Apostles. And he so quotes them, as to intimate that these were the only historical books received by Christians as of authority, and the only authentic memoirs of Jesus Christ, and His Apostles, and the doctrine preached by them. He allows their early date, and even argues for it. He also quotes, or plainly refers to the Acts of the Apostles, to St. Paul's Epistles to the Romans, the Corinthians, and the Galatians. He does not deny the miracles of Jesus Christ, but allows Him to have healed the blind, and the lame, and demoniacs, and walked upon the waves of the sea," (Lardner, Vol. IY. p. 93). It would be easy to cite other heathen writers of antiquity to the same effect; but the most that can be done within the limits of a single discourse is to present a mere illustration of the opinions they entertained.

Neither can anything more be done in noticing the infidel writers who swarmed in Great Britain during the early part of the preceding and the seventeenth century, nearly all of whose books have long been out of print, while the Bible still lives to bless and comfort and guide unnumbered millions. "Who," says Burke, "born within the last forty years, has read one word of Collins, and Toland, and Tindal, and Chubb, and Morgan, and that whole race who called themselves Freethinkers? Who now reads Bolingbroke? Who ever read him through? Ask the booksellers of London what has become of all these lights of the world," (Burke's Reflections. Works, Vol. Y. p. 172). Hume, who seems to have studiously avoided the mention of Jesus' name, at least indirectly admits the practical value of the teachings of Jesus and the Apostles, when he refers to those who "suppose that the Deity will inflict punishments on vice, and bestow rewards on virtue, beyond what appear in the ordinary course of nature," and then adds, "Whether this reasoning of theirs be just or not, is no matter. Its influence on their life and conduct must still be the same: and those who attempt to disabuse them of such prejudices, may, for aught I know, be good reasoners, but I cannot allow them to be good citizens and politicians; since they free men from one restraint upon their passions, and make the infringement of the law of society, in one respect, more easy and secure," (Essays, p. 84).

Hobbes says that though the laws of nature are not laws as they proceed from nature, yet "as they are given by God in holy scripture, they are properly called laws; for the holy scripture is the voice of God, ruling all things by the greatest right," (Leland's Deistical Writers, Vol. I. p. 31). The Earl of Shaftesbury declares that "he who denies a Deity is daringly presumptuous, and sets up an opinion against mankind, and being of society;" and that "nothing can more highly contribute to the fixing of right apprehensions, and a sound judgment, or sense of right and wrong, than to believe a God, who is represented such, as to be a true model or example of the most exalted justice, and highest goodness and worth," (Deistical Writers, Vol. I. p. 79). Lord Bolingbroke affirms that "no system can be more simple and plain than that of natural religion as it stands in the Gospel;" and that "both the duties required to be practiced, and the propositions required to be believed, are concisely and plainly enough expressed in the original Gospel properly so called, which Christ taught, and which his four Evangelists recorded. But they have been alike corrupted by theology," (Deistical Writers, p. 164). Thomas Chubb says, "In Christ we have an example of a quiet and peaceable spirit; of a becoming modesty and sobriety; just, honest, upright, sincere; and, above all, of a most gracious and benevolent temper and behavior. . . . His life was a beautiful picture of human nature in its native purity and simplicity, and showed at once what excellent creatures men would be, when under the influence and power of that Gospel which He preached unto them." The copy of the Deistical Writers in my possession, containing extracts from Chubb's Posthumous Works, has upon the margin in ink the following note which appears to have been written in 1772: "I have been informed on very good authority that Chubb at his death left, signed with his name, a solemn declaration to this purport: 'I am extremely distressed for what I have written against the Christian religion, and implore the Divine forgiveness. I am now fully convinced of the divine authority and truth of Christianity, and in witness hereof I solemnly subscribe my name, Thomas Chubb.' The bookseller who published his Posthumous Works, when this declaration was offered to him, refused to print it, alleging that it would ruin the sale of the copies."

Crossing now the Channel to the Continent, we are met at once by the remarkable and well-known confession of Rousseau, which will surely outlive everything else he wrote: "Peruse the works of our philosophers, with all their pomp of diction, how mean, how contemptible are they, compared with the Scriptures! Is it possible that a book, at once so simple and so sublime, should be merely the work of man? Is it possible that the sacred personage, whose history it contains, should be himself a mere man? Do we find that he assumed the tone of an enthusiast, or an ambitious sectary? What sweetness, what purity, in his manner! What an affecting gracefulness in his instructions! What sublimity in his maxims! What profound wisdom in his discourses! What presence of mind, what subtlety', what fitness in his replies! How great the command over his passions! Where is the man, where the philosopher, who could so live and so die, without weakness, and without ostentation?... Yes, if the life and death of Socrates were those of a sage, the life and death of Jesus are those of a God. Shall we suppose the evangelical history a mere fiction 'I Indeed, my friend, it bears no marks of fiction. On the contrary, the history of Socrates, which no one presumes to doubt, is not so well attested as that of Jesus Christ. Such a supposition, in fact, only shifts the difficulty without obviating it: it is more inconceivable that a number of persons should agree to write such a history, than that one should furnish the subject of it. The Jewish authors were incapable of the diction, and strangers to the morality contained in the gospel. The marks of its truth are so striking and inimitable, that the inventor would be a more astonishing character than the hero," (Emile ou de L'Education).

We come next to the equally remarkable confession of Napoleon Bonaparte, as given by those who were his companions on the island of St. Helena. Of course it is impossible to vouch for the entire correctness of their reports, but it is certain that they endeavored, by comparing notes and their recollections of his remarks, to put these remarks into writing with as much accuracy as possible; and it is also certain that not one of them was capable of making the argument which is ascribed to him, and at which we can only glance. As Schaft says, his reported religious conversations "have the grandiloquent and egotistic Napoleonic ring, and are marked by that massive grandeur and granite-like simplicity of thought and style which characterize the best of his utterances. They are, moreover, quite consistent with the undeniable fact, that he expressed himself, both in his testament and on his death-bed, a believer in the Catholic Christian religion, which always taught the divinity of Christ as a fundamental article of faith." Nothing more than the merest abstract of his statements can be presented now.

General Bertrand having expressed on one occasion his admiration of Jesus as a man, but his belief as to any higher nature, Napoleon replied, "I know men, and I tell you that Jesus Christ is not a man. Superficial minds see a resemblance between Christ and the founders of empires. That resemblance does not exist. There is between Christianity and whatever religion the distance of infinity. . . . Paganism is the work of man. One can here read but our imbecility. What do these gods, so boastful, know more than other mortals? these legislators, Greek or Roman? this Numa? this Lycurgus! these priests of India or of Memphis? this Confucius? this Mohammed? Absolutely nothing. They have made a perfect chaos of morals. There is not one among them all who has said anything new in reference to our future destiny, to the soul, to the essence of God, to the creation. . . . It is not so with Christ. Everything in him astonishes me. His spirit overawes me, and his will confounds me. Between him and whoever else in the world, there is no possible term of comparison. He is truly a being by himself. His ideas, and his sentiments, the truths which he announces, his manner of convincing, are not explained either by human organization or by the nature of things. His birth, and the history of his life; the profundity of his doctrine, which grapples the mightiest difficulties, and which is, of those difficulties, the most admirable solution; his Gospel, his apparition, his empire, his march across the ages and realms, everything, is for me a prodigy, a mystery insoluble, which plunges me into a reverie from which I can not escape, a mystery which is there before my eyes, a mystery which I can neither deny nor explain. Here I see nothing human.

"The nearer I approach, the more carefully I examine, everything is above me, everything remains grand—of a grandeur that overpowers. His religion is a revelation from an intelligence which certainly is not that of man. There is there a profound originality, which has created a series of words and of maxims before unknown. Jesus borrowed nothing from our sciences. . . . I search in vain in history to find the similar to Jesus Christ, or anything which can approach the Gospel. Neither history, nor humanity, nor the ages, nor nature, can offer me anything with which I am able to compare it or explain it. Here everything is extraordinary. The more I consider the Gospel, the more I am assured that there is nothing which is not beyond the march of events and above the human mind. Even the impious themselves have never dared to deny the sublimity of the Gospel, which inspires them with a sort of compulsory veneration. What happiness that book produces for them who believe it! What marvels those admire who reflect upon it! Book unique, where the mind finds a moral beauty before unknown, and an idea of the Supreme superior even to that which creation suggests! Who but God could produce that type, that ideal of perfection, equally exclusive and original?...

"You speak of Caesar, of Alexander, of their conquests, and of the enthusiasm they enkindled in the hearts of their soldiers; but can you conceive of a dead man making conquests with an army faithful and entirely devoted to his memory? My armies have forgotten me, even while living, as the Carthagenian army forgot Hannibal. Such is our power! A single battle lost crushes us, and adversity scatters our friends. Can you conceive of Caesar, the eternal emperor of the Roman senate, and from the depths of his mausoleum governing the empire, watching over the destinies of Rome? . . . Truth should embrace the universe. Such is Christianity, the only religion which destroys sectional prejudice, the only one which proclaims the unity and absolute brotherhood of the whole human family, the only one which is purely spiritual—in line, the only one which assigns to all, without distinction, for a true country the bosom of the Creator, God. Christ proved that he was the son of the Eternal by his disregard of time. All his doctrines signify one only and the same thing—Eternity. It is true that Christ proposed to our faith a series of mysteries. He commands with authority that we should believe them, giving no other reason than those tremendous words, '*I am God*.' He declares it. What an abyss he created by that declaration between himself and all the fabricators of religion! What audacity, what sacrilege, what blasphemy, if it were not true! I say more; the universal triumph of an affirmation of that kind, if the triumph was not really that of God himself, would be a plausible excuse and a reason for atheism." . . . For a moment the Emperor was silent. As General Bertrand made no reply, he solemnly added, "If you do not perceive that Jesus Christ is God, very well, then I did wrong to make you a general," (Life of Napoleon, Vol. II., pp. 612-618.)

The next witness to be summoned is Strauss himself, who will probably be claimed by his admirers as a kind of intellectual Napoleon, performing as many wonders in the field of dialectics as the French Emperor accomplished on the field of battle. In an earlier essay quoted by Schaff, he says, "As little as humanity will ever be without" religion, as little will it be without Christ; for to have religion without Christ would be as absurd as to enjoy poetry without regard to Homer or Shakspeare. And this Christ, as far as he is inseparable from the highest style of religion, is *historically* not mythical; is an *individual*, no mere symbol. To the historical person of Christ belongs all in his life that exhibits his religious perfection, his discourses, his moral action, and his passion. . . . He remains the highest model of religion within the reach of our thought; and no perfect "Deity is possible without his presence in the heart."

Even in his larger and later work he says, "The Roman conceived of man as he ought to be differently from the Greek, the Jew differently from both, the Greek, after Socrates, differently from, and unquestionably more perfectly than before. Every man of moral pre-eminence, every great thinker who has made the active nature of man the object of his investigation, has contributed in narrow or wider circles towards correcting that idea, perfecting or improving it. And among these improvers of the ideal of humanity Jesus stands, at all events, in the first class. He introduced features into it which were wanting to it before, or had continued undeveloped; reduced the dimensions of others which prevented its universal application; imparted into it, by the religious aspect which he gave it, a more lofty consecration, and bestowed upon it, by embodying it in his own person, the most vital warmth; while the

Religious 'Society which took its rise from him provided for this ideal the widest acceptance among mankind," (Vol. II. pp. 436-437).

Appropriately following Strauss, Renan may be called to the stand to express his estimate of Jesus. In opposition to his German friend, he accepts as especially authentic and trustworthy the Gospel of John; and referring to the interview, there recorded, between Jesus and the woman at Sychar's well, when our Lord said to her, "The hour cometh, and now is, when the true worshippers shall worship the Father in spirit and in truth, for the Father seeketh such to worship him," the French infidel says, "On the day when he pronounced these words, he was indeed the son of God. He for the first time gave utterance to the idea upon which shall rest the edifice of the everlasting religion. He founded the pure worship, of no age, of no clime, which shall be that of all lofty souls to the end of time. Not only was his religion, that day, the benign religion of humanity, but it was the absolute religion; and if other planets have inhabitants endowed with reason and morality, their religion can not be different from that which Jesus proclaimed at Jacob's well. Man has not been able to abide by this worship; we attain the ideal only for a moment. The words of Jesus were a gleam in thick night; it has taken eighteen hundred years for the eyes of humanity (what do I say! of an infinitely small portion of humanity) to abide it. But the gleam shall become the full day, and, after passing through all the circles of error, humanity will return to these words, as to the immortal expression of its faith and its hopes," (Life of Jesus, p. 215).

Again, alluding to His death he says, "Repose now in the glory, noble founder. Thy work is finished, thy divinity is established. Fear no more to see the edifice of thy labors fall by any fault. Henceforth, beyond the reach of frailty, thou shalt witness from the heights of divine peace, the infinite results of thy acts. At the price of a few hours of suffering, which did not even reach thy grand soul, thou hast bought the most complete immortality. For thousands of years, the world will depend on thee! Banner of our contests, thou shalt be the standard about which the hottest battle will be given. A thousand times more alive, a thousand times more beloved, since thy death than during thy passage here below, thou shalt become the corner-stone of humanity so entirely, that to tear thy name from this world would be to rend it to its foundations. Between thee and God, there will be no longer any distinction. Complete conqueror of death, take possession of thy kingdom, whither shall follow thee, by the royal road which thou hast traced, ages of worshippers," (Life of Jesus, p. 351). So he closes his rhapsody by saying, "Whatever may be the surprises of the future, Jesus will never be surpassed. His worship will grow young without ceasing; his legend will call forth tears without end; his sufferings will melt the noblest hearts; all ages will proclaim that among the sons of men there is none born greater than Jesus," (p. 376). But even this does not surpass the words of Jean Paul Richter, when speaking of that majestic One who, "being the Holiest among the mighty, and the Mightiest among the holy, has lifted with his pierced hand empires off their hinges, has turned the stream of centuries out of its channel, and still governs the ages."

Surely it is needless to present other quotations, that could be continued indefinitely. The friends and the foes of the crucified Jesus seem to vie with each other in their estimate of His worth, and in their eulogies upon His character. Would this have been possible, if He were an impostor, or a fanatic, or less than supernatural? Has any life been so closely scrutinized! Has any biography been so severely criticised? Would not a hypocrite or a charlatan have been long ago exposed, and dismissed from the attention of thoughtful men with merited contempt? It is vain to reply by referring to the regard with which the names of Mohammed, Confucius, and the authors of the Hindoo Vedas are still cherished in different parts of the earth. Very often noble opinions and sentiments are attributed to these men which they never thought of uttering; and the skeptics who are guilty of this despicable trick in order to cast discredit on the Gospel, if they really have any familiarity with their writings, are careful to conceal from the common people the monstrous errors, and wretched morals, and childish superstitions, and grotesque extravagances with which the heathen writings they profess to admire notoriously abound. This is so well known indeed that any serious attempt to substitute the religion of Mohammed or Confucius or Brahma for Christianity in Europe or the United States would be hailed with a shout of laughter as a ludicrous farce. Whatever they may be to the people of Turkey or China or India, they can never be anything to those who are blessed with the brighter light of Christian civilization. But is this true of Jesus with respect to any nation or race beneath the sun? Is He not precisely adapted to all classes of all climes? May not a Newton and a child bow together at His feet, the accomplished scholar and the untutored savage meet in sweetest sympathy at His cross? Would infidels themselves exchange His Gospel for any other religion? Nay, would they be willing to live, or to have their families live, in a laud or in a community, where His Gospel is wholly unknown, or from which His Gospel has been totally banished? Not one of them, who possesses the lowest degree of intelligence or of respect for morality. A dying infidel said to me not long ago, "I do not wish my children to accept my views;" and probably every thoughtful skeptic would say the same thing, thus bearing testimony again to the high estimate which is somehow put upon the value of Jesus even by those who do not believe on Him as their Redeemer.

There is now in my study, in manuscript, a confession read to a large assembly in Kentucky by a man who had reached his seventy-first birthday. He was a physician of fine culture, possessing ample means and abundant leisure for the gratification of his literary tastes, and standing among his acquaintances even above the breath of reproach or suspicion. For more than sixty years he was an avowed infidel, and no argument the ablest Christians could bring to bear upon his objections to the Bible could move him a hair's breadth from his position of unbelief. His confession begins as follows: "A deist, a skeptic, with a character for integrity, probity and benevolence among men, I was a self-righteous Pharisee. Trusting in my own reason, vaunting my own ability, proud of my reputation, believing in my own worth and merits, I was as one born blind. I was self-deceived, and believed I was doing God's service, when I denied His revealed word, and controverted the truths of Scripture. If I know myself I was honest in my opposition to all supernatural knowledge. I believed that God had revealed Himself in nature, and nowhere else; but that revelation was limited, and, to my mind, unsatisfactory. I knew not what I was doing. I was as those for whom Jesus prayed in His dying agony on the cross, 'Father, forgive them, for they know not what they do.' I, even I, was included in that prayer; and in the blessed Saviour, I, even I, once His enemy, but now His worshipper, 'have an advocate with the Father,' yea, an almighty friend, a mediator and intercessor, through whom I am enabled to say, 'Abba, Father.' Blessed be God for Jesus Christ, the friend and Saviour of sinners!"

That man, before he became a Christian, talked with me by the hour, and sincerely declared that he could see no proof of a divine origin stamped upon the Bible, and no beauty in Jesus that He should be desired. After he became a Christian it was my privilege to meet him again, and, as he approached, the tears were running down his manly face, while he exclaimed with tremulous voice, "Since I saw you last, I have found Jesus unutterably precious to my soul." His daughter, whom he tenderly loved, had died a Christian, and in the darkness of his skepticism, and out of the depth of his grief, he had shrieked, "Where is my child? Is she gone from me forever? Shall I see her no more, no more? Can I never press her to my bosom?" But like Baal, when the false prophets leaped upon the altar, and cut themselves, after their manner, with knives and lancets, till the blood gashed out upon them, "there was no voice, nor any that answered," (1 Kings xviii. 26-28). "Oh, sir," he said, "nature, reason, philosophy, science, were all dumb as the silent grave that held the form of my precious child: and I turned to Jesus, because He alone met and satisfied a great, crying want of my aching heart."

Yes, this is one of the many crowns that adorn the brow of our adorable Lord; He meets our wants, not by the stretch of an excited imagination reaching out to fancied help, but by the actual communications of His grace, as ten thousand times ten thousand truthful witnesses would spring to their feet to testify to-night. Theodore Parker, another infidel of the Strauss or Baur school, speaking of Jesus, said, "That mightiest heart that ever beat, stirred by the Spirit of God, how it wrought in his bosom! What words of rebuke, of comfort, counsel, admonition, promise, hope, did he pour out! -Words that stir the soul as summer dews call up the faint and sickly grass." The time is coming, and coming very soon, dear friends, when the world will present to you but the appearance of faint and sickly grass, and you will thirst for the gentle dews which only Jesus can send. Disappointment in every earthly pursuit is coming, the enforced cessation of business is coming, the desertion of those you trusted is coming, the bitterness of enemies is coming, the deep shadow of a grave, to rest upon your heart and home, is coming, disease is coming, pain is coming, the last look upon the faces of loved ones is coming, the loneliness of the tomb is coming, the vastness of eternity is coming, the judgment day is coming; and in every trying experience you will need just such a friend as Jesus in His human sympathy and divine sufficiency.

"I, if I be lifted up from the earth, will draw all men unto me," (John xii. 32), is His own sublime assertion of the universality of His empire; and are you sure the assertion is not true? Would it not be better for you if drawn "with cords of a man, with bands of love" to dwell amid the pleasures that are at His right hand forevermore, than to be dragged by the chains of unappeased justice, to hear from the lips, that now entreat you, the sentence of a righteous condemnation, "Depart from me!" Do you believe that Christians and intelligent and respectable infidels would have agreed so nearly in their estimate of His person and character, unless He is what He claims to be? But if He is what He claims to be, and of this there are innumerable witnesses, the hour is near when at the mention of His name, heaven shall ring with the hallelujahs of the redeemed, and the shout of angels, and even the confessions of the lost, that Jesus Christ is Lord, to the glory of God the Father. May the admissions of skeptics which you have heard this evening lead you to Him whose word they reject; "for their rock is not as our Rock, even our enemies themselves being judges!" (Deut. xxxii. 31).

CHAPTER 5
THE RESURRECTION OF JESUS

Strauss, in approaching the discussion of this mighty subject, says, "Here then we stand on that decisive point where, in the presence of the accounts of the miraculous resurrection of Jesus, we either acknowledge the inadmissibility of the natural and historical view of the life of Jesus, and must consequently retract all that precedes, and so give up our whole undertaking, or pledge ourselves to make out the possibility of the result of these accounts, *i. e.*, the origin of the belief in the resurrection of Jesus without any corresponding miraculous fact. The more immediately this question touches all Christianity to the quick, the more regard we must pay to the sensibility with which every unprejudiced word that is uttered about it is received, and even to the sensible effect which such words may have upon him who pronounces them; but the more important the point is, and the more decisive on the other side, for the whole view of Christianity, the more pressing is the demand upon the investigator to set aside all these considerations, and pronounce upon it in a perfectly unprejudiced, perfectly decided spirit, without ambiguity and without reserve."

Then, after alluding, with scarcely concealed contempt, to the views of those infidels who hold that the death of Jesus upon the cross was not real, he refers to Baur, his own master in the school of skeptical criticism of which he became the most distinguished representative, and adds, "Even Baur himself has vouchsafed to declare that the real nature of the Resurrection of Jesus lies outside the limits of historical investigation, and has accordingly, at least in words, avoided the burning question. For his words appear to mean that it can not be historically discovered, and that it is not even a problem for historical investigation to find out whether the Resurrection of Jesus was an objective occurrence, either miraculous or natural, or whether it was only the belief of his disciples." In this connection he speaks of "the apologists who would like to persuade the world that if the reality of the Resurrection is not recognized, the origin and rise of the Christian Church can not be explained," and continues: "No, says the historian, and rightly, only this much need be acknowledged, that the disciples firmly believed that Jesus had arisen; this is perfectly sufficient to make their further progress and operations intelligible; what that belief rested upon, what there was real in the resurrection of Jesus is an open question, which the investigator may answer one way or another, without the origin of Christianity being thereby made more or less conceivable." As for himself he can not accept the account given in the New Testament of the resurrection, "but we are prevented," he says, "by various reasons from adopting this view as our own. Whether we consider miracles in general as possible or not, if we are to consider a miracle of so unheard of a description as having really occurred, it must be proved to us by evidence in such a manner, that the untruth of such evidence would be more difficult to conceive than the reality of that which it was intended to prove,"- (Vol. I. pp. 397-398).

With all this the Christian may heartily agree. The literal resurrection of Jesus is indeed the decisive point upon which the whole of our faith turns, upon which the divine origin of the Bible turns, upon which the hope of mankind turns, so far as that hope is shaped by the life, the character, the teachings, the death of Christ; and Strauss well calls it "the burning question." We may even agree, in our anxiety to escape from dispute where it is possible to be avoided, that the origin and rise of the Christian Church can be explained without the necessity of recognizing the reality of the resurrection, if only thus much be acknowledged, that the disciples firmly believed that Jesus had arisen. It is still further agreed that a miracle of so unheard of a description must be proved by evidence in such a manner, that the untruth of such evidence would be more difficult to conceive than the reality of that which it was intended to prove. The argument, then, will rest entirely upon the premises which he lays down, and it is to be regretted that within the limits of a single public discourse he can not be followed step by step, and inch by inch, along the track of his wonderfully subtle reasoning; for it is certain that the heart of the believer would throb with quicker joy on the discovery that, after the utmost resources of human ability and ingenuity have been exhausted in attacking the foundation of his hope, his faith in the resurrection of Jesus stands firmer than ever; and he would surely accord with the judgment given by Schaff, that "the chapter on the resurrection of Jesus is the weakest part of Strauss's book, where his mythological hypothesis breaks down completely," (Person of Christ, p. 165).

It is important at the outset to inform those who have never read his book of his admissions concerning Jesus, admissions that constitute the basis of his argument and are built into the whole structure of his work; and it is fair to add that as it is a work which has never been equalled in the past by the enemies of Christianity, so it will never be surpassed in the future. Infidelity has no weapon left that lies outside the armory of Strauss, or that has not been used in his powerful but ineffectual assault. He admits that such a person as Jesus lived more than eighteen hundred years ago; that He taught very remarkable doctrines touching God and man; that He went about, accompanied by a number of disciples, proclaiming these doctrines, and doing many kind and benevolent acts; that in the course of His brief public career He announced that He was the Messiah mentioned by the Old Testament prophets, and was received as such by His followers; that He thus incurred the enmity of the Jewish rulers, and was at last put to death by order of the Roman governor of Judea, that shortly after His death, His disciples firmly believed that He was risen from the dead, and that He would come again, probably very soon, to establish His kingdom, and to reign over the earth. Upon this last point the admission of Strauss is so striking it must be quoted. Jesus, he says, "speaks in the Gospels not only of his resurrection on the third day, but also of the coming of the Son of man, *i. e.*, of his own second coming at a later though not distant period, when he will appear in the clouds of heaven, in divine glory, and accompanied by angels to awake the dead, to judge the quick and the dead, and to open his kingdom, the kingdom of God or heaven [this lie proves by numerous references]. Here we stand face to face with a decisive point.. The ancient Church clung to this part of the doctrine of Jesus in its literal signification, nay it was properly speaking built upon this foundation, since without the expectation of a near return of Christ no

Christian whatever would have come into existence. For us, on the contrary, Jesus has either no existence at all, or exists only as a human being. To a human being no such thing as he here prophesied of himself could happen. If he did prophecy it of himself and expect it himself, he is for us nothing but a fanatic: if, without any conviction on his own part he said it of himself, he was a braggart and an impostor," (Vol. I. p. 322).

These last few words exhibit the fatal weakness of his book as an argument. He takes it for granted that Jesus was a mere man, and then proceeds to explain away or flatly to deny everything that is inconsistent with his foregone conclusion. He assumes throughout the very point to be proved. For him, no matter what may be said, Jesus has either no existence at all, that is, there is no immortality even for the soul, or He exists only as a human being, and therefore Strauss would not be persuaded, "though one rose from the dead." He insists all the time without the slightest evidence upon forcing One, whom the writers of the New Testament everywhere represent as a supernatural being, into helpless subjection to the laws of nature, as they are called; and hence his objection to the statements of the writers that, when Jesus was risen from the dead. He suffered Himself to be touched, and partook of ordinary food, and also passed through closed doors into the presence of His disciples. "A body," says Strauss, "which can be touched, consequently has power of resistance, can not penetrate through closed doors, *i. e.*, can not have at the same time that power of resistance; as, conversely, a body which penetrates through boards without opposition can have no bones, nor any organ by which to digest bread and fish," (Vol. I. p. 407). Can not even a child of common intelligence perceive that this is a shameful begging of the question in claiming, without a particle of proof, that the risen body of Christ was just like the body of an ordinary being! If Jesus was only a man, the elaborate, and often splendid reasoning of Strauss is indeed unanswerable; but if He was more than man, the stately superstructure of the skeptical critic tumbles about his ears in utter ruins.

That He was more than man has been already proved, and it may be proved again by the evidence of His real resurrection "in such a manner, that the untruth of such evidence would be more difficult to conceive than the reality of that which it was intended to prove."

I. As the argument is addressed, not to the Atheist, but the Theist, it will be admitted that it is a possible thing for God to raise the dead.

Even the impersonal God of the Pantheist, and this is what Strauss seems to have been, may be manifested in the body of a risen man, however extraordinary the occurrence, as well as in any other of His strange and multitudinous forms. Fichte says, "The 'I' is the only object in the universe. 'Self' is the absolute principle of all philosophy. 'I' am the creator of the universe. "I make it to realize my own self-development. The thinking of the mind is the active existence of God—so that man and God are identical. I then am God." Hegel says, "God is a mere process, ever unfolding, realizing himself in the human consciousness. God is the dialectic process of thought. In another aspect, God is nature coming to self-consciousness—the absolute idea." But even if this is true, it will not be denied that God can realize his own self-development in a risen body, and become identical with such a body, and awake to self-consciousness in such a body, as a higher exhibition and outreaching of His infinite sufficiency, not less easily than in the thousand displays He is continually making of Himself above the regular routine of nature's laws. On the very threshold of the discussion, therefore, we meet the skeptic with the pertinent question which Paul put to king Agrippa, "Why should it be thought a thing incredible with you, that God should raise the dead?" (Acts xxvi. 8).

II. It will be admitted that it is a possible thing for competent witnesses to have undoubted evidence of the resurrection of a person from the dead. No one can deny that there would be great danger of deception or delusion in asserting such a fact, for many have mistaken for death only a protracted swoon, or a long continued suspension of the vital powers; and many have supposed and even insisted that their departed friends have actually appeared to them, when they have had no other ground for their belief than the play of an excited imagination. But if a number of credible witnesses were intimately and constantly associated with a person during his life, if they had the most complete and unquestioned proof of his death, and if afterwards they distinctly and repeatedly saw him alive, under circumstances that could leave no room whatever for hallucination, attended by results of the most momentous character, that could not by any ingenuity be explained in any other way than by the genuineness of the resurrection, it is obvious "that the untruth of such evidence would be more difficult to conceive than the reality of that which it was intended to prove." It will not do for the skeptic to reply that it is impossible for the dead to arise, as this is a weak and puerile begging the question, that renders the man who obstinately urges it utterly unworthy of further notice. All will concede that it is impossible for a dead person to come forth from the grave; but it was not impossible for a divine person to arise out of the tomb, nor was it impossible for God to lift the iron crown of death from the brow of His only begotten and well beloved Son.

III. It will be admitted that if competent witnesses of such a fact bear such testimony concerning it, that when carefully sifted and thoroughly tested by friend and foe, it is found to be altogether trustworthy in every respect, we are not only authorized, but morally bound, to receive it as true. The character of the witnesses must be closely scrutinized; they must bear the severest cross-examination without flinching, and without contradicting each other's testimony; they must have their motives and purposes in giving such testimony brought out into the clearest light; and they must submit to the most rigid inquiry with regard to the practical bearing and consequences of their assertion; but if after all this no flaw can be found in their story, the refusal to receive it will prove conclusively that the difficulty in the way of believing the resurrection of Jesus is not found in the head, unless it be the head of an idiot, but in the state of the heart as deceitful above all things, and desperately wicked, as in itself enmity against God. His resurrection as everywhere set forth in the New Testament is not represented as a solitary fact, or as some unaccountable display of almighty power, but it is essentially connected with His high claims, previously noticed; and it forms so exclusively the foundation of every doctrine, every duty, every hope, every joy, held out to us by the sacred writers that, if torn away, the New Testament, the Church for eighteen centuries, Christianity itself, our departed friends, our own aspirations and longings, all, all instantly sink out of sight into profoundest darkness. There is, therefore, the most perfect agreement between His claims and His resurrection, for while he could die as the Son of man. He could not remain under the dominion of death as the Son of God, "because," as Peter says, "it was not possible that he should be holden of it," (Acts ii. 24).

IV. This brings us to glance at the relation between the resurrection of Jesus and the entire Bible, that are so linked together from first to last they must stand or fall together. Going back to the earliest records of the human race we are told that God said to the serpent, elsewhere called the devil and Satan, "I will put enmity between thee and the woman, and between thy seed and her seed [not *man's* seed, it will be observed]: it shall bruise thy head, and thou shalt bruise his heel," (Gen. iii. 15).

From that time the promise of a divine Deliverer is set forth with ever-increasing brightness, in type, in prophecy, and in song; and it is a promise always involving His death and resurrection. For example, in the cure and cleansing of the leper, which could be effected only by the immediate interposition of God, we find that two birds were taken, one of which was killed in an earthen vessel over running water, and the live bird having been dipped in the blood of the slain bird was let go to soar away to heaven, bearing upon its wings, as it were, the token of accomplished sacrifice. (Lev. xiv. 5-7). So on the great day of atonement, two goats were chosen, one of which was slain, and its blood carried by the high priest into the most holy place, was sprinkled upon the mercy seat, and seven times before the mercy seat; and the live goat, having had all the sins and transgressions of Israel imputed to it, typically bore away their guilt, thus picturing the efficacy of the death and resurrection of One who was to die for the sins of the people, and to rise again. Still later we hear this august personage saying to His Father, "Thou wilt not leave my soul in hades [the place of departed spirits]; neither wilt thou suffer thine Holy One to see corruption," (Ps. xvi. 10); and again, "Thy dead men shall live, together with my dead body shall they arise," (Isa. xxvi. 19); and again, "It pleased the Lord to bruise him; he hath put him to grief: when thou shalt make his soul an offering for sin, he shall see his seed, he shall prolong his days, and the pleasure of the Lord shall prosper in his hand. He shall see of the travail of his soul, and shall be satisfied," (Isa. liii. 10, 11).

These are mere illustrations of the general drift of the Old Testament concerning the predicted Messiah who, according to the declarations of the New Testament writers and of Jesus Himself, was held up in symbol to the contemplation of the Jews in all the services of the tabernacle and temple, in events of national importance and in the ordinary incidents of family and individual life, so that He became the sum and the substance, the centre and the circumference of the ancient Scriptures, that have no interest and no significance apart from His anticipated death and resurrection. Moreover the prophets rose to their loftiest and sublimest strains in foretelling, not His sufferings only, when wounded for our transgressions and bruised for our iniquities, but especially in announcing His second advent to earth amid the pomp of supreme royalty and the pageantry of the skies. With this second advent all the hopes of the Hebrews as a people, so marvellously preserved through the ages, are bound up; and it is this alone that throws light upon their strange history, about which Hegel, it is said by his biographer, having often thought, and often changed his thoughts, confessed that "all his life long it tormented him as a dark enigma." It is the time when their banner, that has been trampled in the dust for twenty-five hundred years by the Babylonian, the Persian, the Greek, the Roman, the Mohammedan, and the Gentile world at large, shall float again in triumph from the battlements of Mount Zion; but every one of the many scores of predictions of their present shame is connected with the death of their Messiah, as every prediction of their future glory is connected with His resurrection.

V. Such then to an intelligent faith was the expectation that waited on the coming of the Messiah; and apart from the fact that more than a hundred minute predictions concerning Him are said in the New Testament to have been fulfilled in the person, and ministry, and sufferings of Jesus, we discover that the latter distinctly and repeatedly spoke of His approaching death and resurrection. We need go no further at present than the Gospel of Matthew, which Strauss insists is the most trustworthy, and it is laden with the burden of His coming woe, but light with the victory that would follow. It is easy to perceive that from first to last He walked in the shadow of the cross, which He beheld looming against the sky, but beyond the gloom the future was radiant to His eye with the brightness of resurrection joy. Hence at the very beginning of His ministry He speaks of those who are reviled and persecuted for His sake (Matt. V. 11); of false prophets standing before Him in a day that lies on the other side of death (vii. 22); of taking the cross and following Him even to the grave (x. 38, 39); of continuing three days and three nights in the heart of the earth (xii. 40); and of sending forth His angels in the harvest of the world to gather out of His kingdom all things that offend, and them which do iniquity (xiii. 41). Still more distinctly, when Peter confessed Him to be the Christ, or Messiah, the Son of the living God, "from that time forth began Jesus to show unto his disciples, how that he must go unto Jerusalem, and suffer many things of the elders and chief priests, and scribes, and be killed, and be raised again the third day," (xvi. 21). Again, after the transfiguration, that gave a glimpse of His promised kingdom, while He and the disciples abode in Galilee, "Jesus said unto them. The Son of man shall be betrayed into the hands of men; and they shall kill him, and the third day he shall be raised again," (xvii. 22, 23). This is succeeded by the announcement that those who had followed Him, in the regeneration, when the Son of man shall sit upon the throne of His glory, should also sit upon twelve thrones judging the twelve tribes of Israel (xix. 28); and this by another distinct statement that "Jesus going up to Jerusalem, took the twelve disciples apart in the way, and said unto them, Behold, we go up to Jerusalem; and the Son of man shall be betrayed unto the chief priests and unto the scribes, and they shall condemn him to death, and shall deliver him to the Gentiles, to mock, and to scourge, and to crucify him: and the third day he shall rise again," (xx. 17, 19).

Then comes the prediction of His death, as the Son of God, in the parable of the vineyard (xxi. 37-39); then His defence of the doctrine of the resurrection against the Sadducees in His significant reproof, "Ye do err, not knowing the scriptures, nor the power of God," and in the sublime declaration, "God is not the God of the dead, but of the living," (xxii. 29,32); then his sorrowful farewell to Jerusalem, whose children should see Him no more, till they would say in the extremity of their distress, "Blessed is he that cometh in the name of the Lord," (xxiii. 37-39); then two entire chapters declaring that immediately after a tribulation yet future, of which the destruction of the sacred city by Titus was a faint type, "shall all the tribes of the earth mourn, and they shall see the Son of man coming in the clouds of heaven, with power and great glory," (xxiv. 30); that when His Church is wrapped in the deep sleep of spiritual insensibility, at midnight a cry shall be heard, "Behold, the bridegroom cometh; go ye out to meet him," (xxv. 6); that during the period of His absence from the earth He commits certain talents to His servants, and "after a long time, the lord of those servants cometh, and reckoneth with them," (xxv. 19); that "when the Son of man shall come in his glory, and all the holy angels with him, then shall he sit upon the throne of his glory: and before him shall be gathered all nations," (xxv. 31); then His solemn testimony at His trial before the high priest, when put upon His oath, or adjured by the living God to say plainly whether He was the Christ, the Son of God, "I am," as Mark has it, and "hereafter shall ye see the Son of man sitting on the right hand of power, and coming in the clouds of heaven," (xxvi. 64); then the account of His death, followed by the statement that when His body was in the grave, "the chief priests and Pharisees came together unto Pilate, saying. Sir, we remember that that deceiver said, while lie was yet alive, After three days I will rise again," and procuring a band of soldiers to watch the tomb, "lest his disciples come by night, and steal him away, and say unto the people, He is risen from the dead; so the last error shall be worse than the first," (xxvii. 62-66); and then the narrative of His resurrection and His subsequent appearance to the disciples (xxviii). Such is an imperfect outline of the references to the resurrection contained in the Gospel of Matthew, which, you must remember, Strauss regards as the most trustworthy. These references are so interwoven with the entire structure of the book that, if removed, there would be no Gospel by Matthew; and although Jesus, in prophesying such things of Himself, may be for Strauss nothing but a fanatic, or a braggart and an imposter, still it is certain that He did repeatedly and constantly prophesy such things of Himself according to the testimony of one whom Strauss recognizes as the most trustworthy witness. It does not concern us to know what opinion Strauss chose to entertain of the character of Jesus, but it does concern us to know that Jesus plainly and frequently predicted His resurrection.

VI. This is a suitable connection in which to notice the various accounts of the resurrection, as given by Matthew, Mark, Luke, and John. Would that there was time to take up one by one the charges which Strauss brings of conflicting and contradictory testimony in these accounts, that as his charges are confuted and completely swept away, the hearts of Christians might burn within them, like the hearts of the two disciples walking to Emmaus, when the risen Jesus talked with them by the way, and while He opened to them the scriptures. The mistake of Strauss and all his class of writers in dealing with the accounts of the resurrection. consists in their failure to see the different design of the Holy Ghost in each of the four Gospels, or, if this expression offends them, the different purposes of the four human writers. Thus it is apparent to all who have really studied the Gospels, that it was the purpose of Matthew to set forth Jesus specially in His relation to the Jews as the son of David, and son of Abraham, and Lion of the tribe of Judah, disowned and rejected indeed, and going out in grace to meet the need of sinful Gentiles. It was the purpose of Mark to proclaim Him as the obedient servant, prompt to do God's bidding, coming, not to be ministered unto, but to minister. It was the purpose of Luke to reveal Him in His broadest aspects as the Son of man; and it was the purpose of John to show Him to the world as the Son of God, the heavenly stranger, tarrying a little while on earth to die, that whosoever believeth on Him may not perish, but have everlasting life, and then returning to the bosom of the Father.

Hence it was not the wish of either to furnish a complete narrative of the resurrection, or of many other facts in the life of our Lord, but only the features that were in accordance with the aim of each book; and this is found upon examination to be true in their accounts of the resurrection which, however diversified in certain details, and independent in one sense, are in perfect harmony with each other, and with the end each writer had in view in preparing his particular history. But would it not have been an easy task to make their accounts precisely similar in every respect? One of these books was written before the others, Matthew, the most trustworthy, according to Strauss, being the first, and as previously shown, it was soon publicly read at least once every week in a multitude of congregations. When Mark, Luke, and John subsequently concluded, speaking after the manner of men, to furnish their own narratives, it would have been a very simple thing, which a child could accomplish, to copy word for word, the account already given by Matthew. Yet if this had been done, what a howl would have been raised by infidelity, calling attention to the positive proof of collusion and forgery! As it was not done, infidelity turns upon you with the assertion that the accounts contain contradictory testimony, showing how utterly impossible it is to satisfy a skeptical spirit, no matter what the Bible says. But even the most skeptical spirit will be compelled to admit that the four Gospels precisely agree in all the leading facts connected with the resurrection. They all agree in asserting the real death of Jesus on the Cross. They all agree in saying that His body was buried in the tomb of Joseph of Arimathea, with whom, John adds, Nicodemus also came, having obtained permission from Pilate to dispose of the remains; for as Strauss says, "there was a Roman law which gave the bodies of criminals so executed to their relations or friends, if they themselves asked for them," (Vol. I. p. 396). They all agree in regard to the statement that certain women went first to the sepulchre early on the morning of the first day of the week; they all agree that these women found the stone rolled away from the mouth of the sepulchre, and the sepulchre itself empty; and they all agree that the resurrection had previously occurred; though no one of them tells us that any mortal eye saw Him rise, nor do they inform us as to the manner of His resurrection, which they would surely have done, if the story had been an invention of their own.

Let us now bring these separate accounts together in their minutest particulars, and see whether Christians will not have occasion to admire and adore the divine wisdom and love that so marvellously protected the obviously honest narratives against every theory which would deny their perfect credibility. Jesus hanging on the cross, having cried, not with a faint voice indicating a swoon, but with a loud voice, "Father, into thy hands I commend my spirit," bowed His head, and gave up the ghost. It was about the ninth hour, or three o'clock in the afternoon of Friday, that is, three hours before the commencement of the Jewish Sabbath. Because it was the preparation, soldiers came at the request of the Jewish rulers, and with the consent of Pilate, to hasten the death of the three who were crucified, and who might have lingered in their agony for a day or two; but finding that Jesus was already dead, they brake not his legs, though one of the soldiers with a spear pierced his side, making his death doubly sure. Immediately afterwards, Joseph of Arimathea arrived, and with the assistance of Nicodemus, took down the body, and having wrapped it in a linen cloth, with such perfumes as the latter brought, he placed it, Matthew says, in his own new tomb, which Mark tells us was hewn out of a rock, and Luke and John add, "wherein never man before was laid." Matthew and Mark state that Mary Magdalene, and Mary, the mother of James and Joses, among other women, beheld where He was laid, while Luke describes them as the women "which came with him from Galilee," and also states that they returned to the city, "and prepared spices and ointments, and rested the sabbath day, according to the commandment." The first day of the week, very early in the morning according to Luke, when it was yet dark according to John, as it began to dawn according to Matthew, these women came, bringing the spices they had prepared as Mark and Luke assert, Mark telling us that though it was very early in the morning when they left home, they came unto the sepulchre at the rising of the sun, and we know how brief is the interval in that latitude between the dawn and the morning. John mentions only Mary Magdalene, but he states that when she saw the empty sepulchre, she ran at once to Peter and John, who are always represented as intimately associated, exclaiming, "They have taken away the Lord out of the sepulchre, and ice know not where they have laid him." She did not say; I know not, but we know not, furnishing the strongest, because unintentional, evidence that other women were with her. It is pitiful weakness on the part of Strauss, utterly unworthy of his tine intellect, to accuse the four Evangelists of contradicting each other, because they do not mention the same number of women, or of angels, or because Matthew speaks of the angel that sat on the stone at the time of the earthquake, and Mark describes him as sitting in the sepulchre when the women entered. Four Americans on a visit to London might see the Queen accompanied by her children and officers riding in state through the streets on some occasion of national interest. One of them might write home saying that the Queen had appeared on the streets; another that the Queen and the Prince of Wales had appeared; another that the Queen and the Prince and Princess had appeared; another that the royal household had appeared; but there would be no contradiction in their testimony unless one or the other of the writers should affirm that *only* those they had chosen to name had been seen.

So it is here. John speaks of Mary Magdalene; Matthew speaks of Mary Magdalene, and the other Mary; Mark speaks of Mary Magdalene, and Mary the mother of James, and Salome; Luke speaks of Mary Magdalene, and Joanna, and Mary the mother of James, and other women that were with them; and there is no contradiction whatever. The same remark may be made concerning the angels who are represented as appearing at different times and places in connection with the momentous event, now sitting on the stone, then in the sepulchre, then speaking to the women. The same remark may be made about the actions of the women, for Mary ran back to the disciples the moment she perceived that Jesus was not in the sepulchre, while the others remained and saw the angels. Peter and John at once proceeded with her, the latter outrunning the former, and, looking into the empty sepulchre, believed; but the former was simply perplexed, and wondering in himself, departed. Luke mentions only Peter, but he does not say that John was not with him, nor does he say that Peter did not visit the sepulchre twice that great morning, as he probably did at the time the Lord appeared to him alone. Meanwhile the other women having fled in terror, speaking to no one by the way, but hurrying at once to the disciples, Mary stood without weeping, and it was during this second visit Jesus appeared to her, as He was in the act of ascending to the Father. The disciples generally regarded the words of the women, who reported the vision of angels, as idle tales, and two of them immediately left the city for the village of Emmaus, not having received the latest intelligence. But at least one of the women had returned to the sepulchre, and in company with Mary Magdalene was coming into the city the second time when Jesus met them, saying, "All hail!" and permitted them to fall at His feet and worship Him. Even then the disciples believed not, nor would they credit His resurrection until He had appeared to the entire number.

But surely it is needless to push this investigation farther. If any honest inquirer after truth will take four Bibles and, opening to the accounts of the resurrection, will place them side by side, carefully comparing them in all their details, he will soon become convinced that the apparent discrepancies are easily reconciled, and that too by no forced interpretation, nor by the suppression of a single fact recorded in any of the narratives. Nay, the transparent candor and perfect credibility of each writer, and the entire freedom, that is manifest, from all straining at effect and all anxiety as to the reception of the story, will grow upon him with increasing power, and he will say to himself again and again, it is absolutely impossible that these narratives could have been the inventions of forgery, or the products of an excited imagination, for the art required to produce them would be in itself something supernatural. They are narratives which for eighteen hundred years have been most closely and critically scanned by thousands, and tens of thousands, and hundreds of thousands, of the ablest minds of Christendom, for it is by no means true that all the intellectual greatness and honesty and learning belong to the infidels, and not only have these minds failed to discover the slightest discrepancy in the accounts of the resurrection, but they have studied them year after year with an ever-deepening impression of their truth and beauty and divinity. Especially have they poured out unto God the sacrifice of gladness and gratitude, when they have found in the Gospel history of the resurrection of Jesus, at once so simple and so sublime, the crowning proof of His rightful claims upon their confidence and love, the sure evidence of their eternal oneness with a risen Christ, and the strong foundation of every doctrine taught, and every duty enjoined, and every hope held forth in the New Testament.

VII. The statement just made will be fully confirmed if we look for a moment at the use of the resurrection of Jesus made by the Apostles. It will be seen that every doctrine, every duty, and every hope, are so intimately blended with the fact of His resurrection, that the denial of the latter leads to the instant and total annihilation of the former. Of this Strauss takes no notice whatever, and yet every one must perceive that it is too important to be overlooked. Thus the opening statement of the book called "The Acts of the Apostles" assures us that the risen Jesus showed Himself to His disciples, or as the Greek word properly means,

He demonstrated Himself to be alive after His passion, by many infallible proofs, being seen of them forty days, and speaking of the things pertaining to the kingdom of God. This is followed by the statement that when He had given His last command to His disciples, while they beheld, He was taken up, and a cloud received Him out of their sight, and this again by the statement that in the selection of one to take the place of Judas, it was an essential qualification of an Apostle that he must be a personal witness with the others of the resurrection of Jesus, (Acts i. 3, 9, 22). In the next chapter, recording the transactions that occurred on the day of Pentecost, we find Peter with the eleven standing in Jerusalem, where fifty days before Jesus had been put to death, and charging the Jews with the crime of having crucified and slain Him, "whom God hath raised up, having loosed the pains of death; because it was not possible that he should be holden of it; . . . this Jesus hath God raised up, whereof we are all witnesses," (Acts ii. 24, 32). Was there any denial of the bold charge! Was there any attempt to rebut the positive testimony, where it could have been so readily disproved, if it were untrue? Not the slightest; but on the other hand the record states, and its correctness has never been questioned, that three thousand of the Jews, pierced to the heart with conviction, were then and there baptized in the name of the risen Jesus. Why did not the rulers of the Jews expose the body of Jesus, and thus crush Christianity with a blow? Or why did they not prove that the witnesses to the resurrection had stolen the body? Or why did these witnesses, but a few days before, according to their own admission, so discouraged and desponding that they fled like a flock of frightened sheep, suddenly stand forth with an audacity that has never been equalled to assert, not in some distant corner of the land, but in the very city where Jesus had been crucified, His resurrection from the dead? The whole scene is inconceivable and impossible, if the Apostles did not only firmly believe, but knew, that He was actually risen.

In the next chapter we find Peter and John saying to the Jewish rulers, "Ye denied the Holy One and the Just, and desired a murderer to be granted unto you, and killed the Prince of life, whom God hath raised from the dead; whereof we are witnesses," (Acts iii. 14, 15). In the next chapter they say, "Be it known unto you all, and to all the people of Israel, that by the name of Jesus Christ of Nazareth', whom ye crucified, whom God raised from the dead, even by him doth this man stand before you whole," (Acts iv. 10). In the next chapter Peter and the other

Apostles say to the Sanhedrim, "The God of our fathers raised up Jesus, whom ye slew and hanged on a tree. Him hath God exalted with his right hand to be a Prince and a Saviour, for to give repentance to Israel, and forgiveness of sins," (Acts v. 30, 31). Can any one believe that they would have spoken in this manner to their own civil and ecclesiastical rulers, unless they knew that the ground on which they stood was unassailable? But it would be wearisome, if not unprofitable, to continue these quotations, when chapter after chapter brings out the same thing over and over again. If we look at Peter preaching to the Roman centurion in Caesarea, he tells him that the Apostles are witnesses of all things which Jesus did, "whom they slew and hanged on a tree; Him God raised up the third day, and showed him openly," (Acts x. 40). If we look at Paul preaching to the Jews at Antioch in Pisidia, he tells them of Jesus, and says, "God raised him from the dead: and he was seen many days of them which came up with him from Galilee to Jerusalem, who are his witnesses unto the people," (Acts xiii. 30, 31). Or if we look at Paul preaching to the cultivated Athenians on Mars' Hill, he tells them of "Jesus and the resurrection," adding that God "hath appointed a day, in the which he will judge the world in righteousness, by that man whom he hath ordained: whereof he hath given assurance unto all men, in that he hath raised him from the dead," (Acts xvii. 18, 31). Or if we look at Paul preaching in chains to King Agrippa, imprisoned, as the Roman Festus explained to his royal guest, on account of certain questions which the Jews had "against him of their own superstition, and of one Jesus, which was dead, whom Paul affirmed to he alive," (Acts XXV. 19), we find him testifying that he said "none other things than those which the prophets and Moses did say should come: that Christ should suffer, and that he should be the first that should rise from the dead," and moreover affirming that "this thing was not done in a corner," and so powerfully affecting his distinguished auditor that "Agrippa said unto Paul, Almost thou persuadest me to be a Christian," (Acts xxvi. 22-28). Again let the question be asked, can any one believe that Paul would have made such an assertion, in such a presence, unless lie not only firmly believed, but *knew* whereof he affirmed? Would it not have been instantly contradicted and disproved, leaving Paul convicted as an impostor or as insane? Everywhere in the preaching of the Apostles, the resurrection of Jesus, not as a fancy which they fondly cherished, but as a fact of which they were competent witnesses, was their unvarying theme to the high and the low, to the rich and the poor, to the king and the peasant, to the philosopher and the child, to the Jew and the Gentile.

But this is not all, nor the half. It is indissolubly linked with every part and particular of the Christian faith. (1) It is an essential element of the Gospel. "I declare unto you," says Paul, "the gospel which I preached unto you," and then he defines the gospel; "for I delivered unto you first of all that which I also received, how that Christ died for our sins according to the scriptures; and that he was buried, and that he rose again the third day according to the scriptures," (1 Cor. xv. 1-4); "Remember that Jesus Christ, of the seed of David, was raised from the dead according to my gospel," (2 Tim. ii. 8). (2) It is essential to our salvation. "If thou shalt confess with thy mouth the Lord Jesus, and shalt believe in thine heart that God hath raised him from the dead, thou shalt be saved," (Rom. x. 9). (3) It is essential to our justification. Righteousness shall be imputed to us also, "if we believe on him that raised up Jesus our Lord from the dead; who was delivered for our offences, and raised again for our justification," (Rom. iv. 24 25). (4) It is essential to our sanctification. "Therefore we are buried with him by baptism into death: that like as Christ was raised up from the dead by the glory of the Father, even so we also should walk in newness of life: . . . . Knowing that Christ, being raised from the dead, dieth no more; death hath no more dominion over him; . . . Wherefore, my brethren, ye also are become dead to the law by the body of Christ; that ye should be married to another, even to him who is raised from the dead, that we should bring forth fruit unto God," (Rom. vi. 4-9; vii. 4). (5) It is essential to our consecration. "The love of Christ constraineth us; because we thus judge, that if one died for all, then were all dead: and that he died for all, that they which live should not henceforth live unto themselves, but unto him which died for them, and rose again," (2 Cor. v. 14, 15; "for to this end Christ both died, and rose, and revived, that he might be Lord both of the dead and living," (Rom. xiv. 9); "If ye then be risen with Christ, seek those things which are above, where Christ sitteth on the right hand of God," (Col. iii. 1). (6) It is essential to our safety. "Who is he that condemneth? It is Christ that died, yea, rather, that is risen again," (Rom. viii. 34); "God, who is rich in mercy, for his great love wherewith he loved us, even when we were dead in sins, hath quickened us together with Christ, (by grace ye are saved;) and hath raised us up together," (Eph. ii. 4-6); "Buried with him in baptism, wherein also ye are risen with him through the faith of the operation of God, who hath raised him from the dead," (Col. ii. 12). (7) It is essential to our hope. "Blessed be the God and Father of our Lord Jesus Christ, which according to his abundant mercy hath begotten us again to a lively hope by the resurrection of Jesus Christ from the dead," (1 Pet. i. 3). (8) It is essential to our own resurrection. "If the Spirit of him that raised up Jesus from the dead dwell in you, he that raised up Christ from the dead shall also quicken your mortal bodies by his Spirit that dwelleth in you," (Rom. viii. 11); "For if we believe that Jesus died and rose again, even so them also which sleep in Jesus will God bring with him," (1 Thess. iv. 14); "Every man in his own order; Christ the first fruits; afterward they that are Christ's, at his coming," (1 Cor. xv. 23). Such are mere examples of the way in which the resurrection of Jesus is presented throughout the New Testament; and even in the closing book, acknowledged by Strauss to be the genuine work of John, He is everywhere described as risen, and ascended, and swaying the sceptre of empire amid the storms that shall shake the pillars of the earth in the last and perilous days, and coming again with clouds, when "every eye shall see him, and they also which pierced him," (Rev. i. 7). Take away the literal resurrection of Jesus from the Bible, and as Renan says about the consequences of His removal from humanity and the world, you will rend it to its foundations.

VIII. The resurrection of Jesus, thus proclaimed all through the Bible, from the first of Genesis to the last of Revelation, could not possibly have been a myth, but must have been a real, and historical fact. A myth is the representation of a religious truth in the form of a fictitious narrative, but without any consciousness of the difference between them; and Strauss labors hard to prove that there was no objective occurrence which gave rise to the belief in the resurrection of Jesus, which he admits the Apostles firmly held, but only a subjective impression produced on their minds by a vision which they imagined they had seen. With due respect for one whose intellect we are compelled to admire, it may be safely said that a more absurd conceit was never hatched outside the brain of a madman. A number of men who did not exhibit a single trait of fanaticism, possessing none of its credulity, extravagance, ignorance, rashness, self-conceit, who were manifestly calm, cool, collected, judicious, giving to the world confessedly the noblest code of morals it has ever known, imparting the most exalted and the most rational conceptions of God, leaving on record commands and precepts affecting all the relations of life that even the bitterest skeptic acknowledges are eminently wise, and all of which are based on the reality of the resurrection of Jesus, who say of themselves that at the time of His death they obstinately and utterly rejected the first reports of His resurrection, went all over the world asserting that they saw Him after His resurrection, that they saw Him repeatedly, that they saw Him in the day time, that He spoke to them again and again, directing them how to proceed in their work, that He breathed upon them, saying, Receive ye the Holy Ghost, that He ate with them, that He showed them the print of the nails in His hands and of the spear wound in His side, that He demonstrated Himself to be alive after His passion by many infallible proofs during the space of more than a month, and that, they beheld Him visibly ascending to heaven; and yet Strauss gravely asks us to believe that all this was a fancy, a dream, a delusion!

But on the theory that the resurrection was a myth it is simply impossible to account for the conduct of one of these witnesses, who, for a considerable period after the death of Jesus, was not only an unbeliever, but a ferocious persecutor of His disciples. This man, on one of his persecuting excursions, as he drew near to Damascus, was suddenly arrested, as he declares, by a great light from heaven flashing about him at mid-day, and by the sound of a voice saying in articulate language, "Saul, Saul, why persecutest thou me!" Overwhelmed with amazement and awe, he replied, "Who art thou?" when again came the audible words, "I am Jesus, whom thou persecutest." It is childish in Strauss to attempt to set aside the credibility of the narrative, because in one account it is said, that the men which journeyed with Saul stood speechless, hearing a voice but seeing no man, and in another account that they saw indeed the light, and were afraid, but they heard not the voice. It is Luke who gives, in the words of Paul, both accounts, and surely it would have been easy enough for him to avoid the contradiction if any had existed. But he speaks after the manner of the Bible, that always recognizes the difference between the circumcised and uncircumcised ear, and it is obvious that he means to say, his companions heard the sound, but did not understand the words that were uttered, just as Jesus a little while before His death heard the voice of His Father, articulately saying, "I have both glorified it, and will glorify it again," while the people that stood by, and heard it, said that it thundered, (John xii. 28, 29). This explanation is fully confirmed by the meaning of the Greek word, which implies both "to perceive sound," and "to understand." If the narrative is not true, why did not some of the soldiers who travelled with him contradict it? Why did Ananias come on the strength of Paul's myth to this arch enemy of Christianity? Why did Paul challenge investigation both before the whole multitude of Jews in Jerusalem, (Acts xxii.), and before king Agrippa, (Acts xxvi.); and above all, why did Paul become a Christian and constantly affirm that he had seen the risen Jesus? "Am I not an apostle? am I not free? have I not seen Jesus Christ our Lord?" (1 Cor. ix. 1). Baur, the teacher of Strauss, at the close of his long and critical studies, honestly confessed that the conversion of Paul was a mystery which could be explained only by "the miracle of the resurrection," (Christianity and the Christian Church in the First Three Centuries, p. 45). It is not unkind to say that if Strauss had been as magnanimous as he was able, he would have made the same confession, and so given up his whole undertaking; for the untruth of such evidence is surely more difficult to conceive than the reality of that which it was intended to prove.

Hear this last, and in some respects, most important witness, in the Epistle to the Corinthians, which Strauss and all other skeptical critics acknowledge to be genuine. After stating that the resurrection of Jesus is a fundamental part of the gospel, he says, "He was seen of Cephas, then of the twelve: after that, he was seen of above five hundred brethren at once; of whom the greater part remain unto this present [about thirty years after], but some are fallen asleep. [Did they all have a vision, or dream, or mere subjective impression without any objective fact to justify it, and all at the same time?] After that, he was seen of James; then of all the apostles. And last of all he was seen of me also, as of one born out of due time," (1 Cor. XV. 5-8). Here then according to the testimony of a man whose honesty only a fool or a knave can question, in an Epistle of undisputed authenticity, we have a number of appearances, which added to those in the four Gospels and Acts, make at least twelve, under circumstances that utterly preclude the idea of myth. Rejecting the literal resurrection, there is no alternative but the conclusion that Paul and the other Apostles were deliberate and wilful liars, and this conclusion is so monstrous it is scorned even by skeptics who pretend to any decency. No wonder, therefore, Paul adds, "If Christ be not risen, then is our preaching vain, and your faith is also vain. Yea, and we are found false witnesses of God; because we have testified of God that he raised up Christ: whom he raised not up, if so be that the dead rise not. For if the dead rise not, then is not Christ raised: and if Christ be not raised, your faith is vain; ye are yet in your sins. Then they also which are fallen asleep in Christ are perished," (1 Cor. xv. 14-18).

Yes, they are perished, and we too must soon lie down in the dust, not only beside a dead Christ, bat beside a dead Christianity, a dead Bible, a dead world. We look up in our helplessness for help, but there is no living and personal God to meet our cry of agony with a fatherly response, or to bend the laws of nature even once before the expression of His infinite love. He is not the kind Master, but the bound slave of His own laws; and under His government darkness is superior to the One who announced that He was the "Light;" the chains of the lost are stronger than the One who proclaimed that He was the "Way;" falsehood is mightier than the One who declared He was the "Truth;" and death has conquered Him who is everywhere revealed in the Gospels as the "Life." If the resurrection of Jesus is a myth, all the teachings of the scriptures that rest upon it are myths, all the faith* and courage and endurance of the martyrs are myths, all the achievements of His disciples are myths, all the benevolence, all the charity, all the victory gained over selfishness and sin, all the stimulus to human enterprise, all the alleviation of human sorrow, all the history of the race for fifteen hundred years, all the guidance in perplexity, all the solace in affliction, all the hope in living, all the triumph iu dying, known by countless millions, all, all are myths, and Jesus Himself is a myth.

"But now IS Christ risen from the dead, and become the first fruits of them that slept;" for as Beyschlag has well said, "it is infinitely easier to admit that the Christian Church is the offspring of a miracle, than to imagine it born of a lie." The miracle of His resurrection is the earnest and forerunner of even a grander and vaster miracle, when His glad shout shall ring through the silence of the tomb, and a great multitude that no man can number, coming forth in glorious, powerful, and immortal bodies, shall be caught up in clouds with living saints, changed in a moment, to meet Him in the air; "and so shall we ever be with the Lord. Wherefore comfort one another with these words." If it please Him to tarry yet longer, the believer will soon enter the grave, as a quiet resting place from the strife and toil of earth; but his Christian friends can gather around it to lift the Hymn of Praise,

"Thou hast been here, Lord Jesus!
 But Thou art here no more;
The terror and the darkness,

    The night of death, are o'er.
Great Captain of salvation!
    Thy triumphs now we sing;
O Grave, where is thy victory?
    O Death, where is thy sting?"

CHAPTER 6
THE BIBLE ITS OWN WITNESS

Not long since a Christian was requested to name the best book on the "Divine Origin of the Bible." His instant answer was, "The Bible." This is so true it almost justifies the remark of Coleridge that the book most needed is one which will defend Christianity against its defenders. No writer probably has ever undertaken to set forth the claims of the Sacred Scriptures upon the faith and veneration of men, without a humiliating consciousness, not only of his total failure to present them in their full light, but of his own inability to comprehend their breadth and length and depth and height. Or if in a silly conceit of his sufficiency for the task, he has no such consciousness, others are sure to detect his failure for him; for they speedily discover that in comparison with what might have been said and ought to have been said, his brightest arguments are but as the flash of the fire-fly attempting to impart some conception of the sun shining in his strength. Hence the certainty with which every published work on the "Evidences of Christianity "is pronounced by thoughtful and thorough students of the Bible to be unsatisfactory. The reason for this judgment, so uniformly rendered, lies in the vastness of the subject, which is seen only by thoughtful and thorough students. The child looks up at the stars, and imagines that they are very small and within reach of its tiny grasp; but the astronomer walks amid these countless worlds scattered throughout illimitable space, until his spirit is overwhelmed within him. The illiterate rustic ploughs the ground with no knowledge of the earth beneath the fertile soil and the loose stones that are found upon the surface; but to the eye of the geologist the successive strata reveal wondrous secrets, and force him to exclaim, if his sense keeps pace with his science, "Lord, thou hast been our dwelling place in all generations. Before the mountains were brought forth, or ever thou hadst formed the earth and the world, even from everlasting to everlasting thou art God," (Ps. xc. 1, 2). In like manner, precisely in proportion to the infidel's ignorance of the Bible, will be his confidence that it is unworthy of belief; and precisely in proportion to the Christian's acquaintance with the Bible, will be his conviction that none but God could be its author, so that at each step of his investigation he will turn to its defenders, and say in the language the queen of Sheba addressed to Solomon, "Howbeit I believed not the words, until I came, and mine eyes had seen it; and, behold, the half was not told me," (1 Kings x. 7).

The evidence that the Bible is from God is of the same character that proves the material creation to be from God, and it would be as difficult to convince an intelligent believer that the former is the work of man, as to convince him that the latter is the work of chance, or of the blind laws of nature. But with the former as with the latter, it is impossible to describe all the tokens and demonstrations of a divine authorship that are suggested to the mind, because they are innumerable, and are ever increasing with increasing knowledge and observation. As Bacon says in his Advancement of Learning, "it is an assured truth, and a conclusion of experience, that a little or superficial knowledge of philosophy may incline the mind of man to atheism, but a farther proceeding therein doth bring the mind back again to religion;" and to this it may be added that " a farther proceeding therein doth bring the mind "to a recognition of its own weakness when surrounded by the imposing symbols of Jehovah's presence. It is well known that Sir Isaac Newton, when complimented on his matchless attainments in science, declared he was like a little child picking up a few pebbles on the beach, while the shoreless ocean of truth rolled before him unexplored; and that Sir W. Jones, the most accomplished scholar of his day in England, stated that if he had his life to go over he would study nothing but the Epistles of St. Paul. This may appear extravagant to those who casually read the Bible, but it will not seem strange to any who "search the scriptures," as Jesus commands. At the close of the longest and most laborious scrutiny of these ancient writings, the first of which antedates by a thousand years the period of Homer, who is called "the Father of History," the ablest mind will confess that it was just beginning, as it were, to get a glimpse of their infinite meaning.

It has often occured that men have set about their careful examination with the avowed design of disproving their supernatural origin, and have progressed but a little way before bowing in lowly adoration at the voice of God speaking to them in this marvellous book. It is true that many have perused them without any such result, for, as Henry Rogers says, "the works alone that have been written against them would make a library far greater than all the literature of Greece and Rome, taken many times over;" but still the fact remains to be explained that in the face of the most savage criticism which has subjected them to a severer ordeal than any other, and all other, writings in the world, multitudes of all ages and now of all nations, including among them the strongest intellects, have clung with unyielding tenacity to the belief that they are divinely inspired. If it is so easy, as infidelity constantly asserts, to show that they are unworthy of serious attention, how is it that they have made all this stir, and why is it that millions not only in past centuries, but millions living to-day, the equals, to say the least, in character and culture of unbelievers, have persisted in the assertion that they recognize the imprint of the Creator's hand in the volume that is dearer to them than life? Perhaps the following considerations may help to account for the wide-spread faith that it can not be regarded as the invention of man.

I. It will be admitted by all who believe in the existence of a personal God, that He might, if He chose, have given us a written revelation of Himself and of our duty, as well as a revelation of Himself and of our obligations in the works of nature, and by means of the human reason and conscience. It is not here asserted that He has given a written revelation, or that there is any need of such a revelation; but surely it will not be denied that He who made the mind of man, and endowed him with reason and conscience, could communicate His pleasure and His purposes through the agency of human thoughts and words, if He desired to employ them in this service. Every day and every hour we find men controlling the opinions and shaping the conduct of other men by their thoughts expressed in words spoken or written; and beyond all question, God is able to influence the minds of any number He may select to manifest His will.

II. It will be admitted that we can obtain a much clearer and more simple, and therefore more satisfactory knowledge of Him, and of what we ought to do, by a written revelation, than by the displays of His attributes and perfections on the wide field of the material universe, and in the decisions of our own judgment of right and wrong. Or if this is going too far, it will certainly be conceded that for the great mass of mankind, those who have no capacity and no leisure and no inclination for close observation and profound investigation, it is much easier to arrive at some knowledge of the being and character of God, and of the proper standard of morals, by a written revelation, than by a process of diligent and personal inquiry into natural and mental and moral science. The story told of Thales, one of the seven wise men of Greece, illustrates the truth that we can not by searching find out the Almighty unto perfection, for it is said that after repeated attempts to define God, he confessed he was further from success at the end than at the commencement of his efforts. Plato, speaking of the soul in its relations to eternity, and of the rule of right for its government here, says "The truth is, to determine anything certain about these matters, in the midst of so many doubts and disputations, is the work of God only." Again, he represents Socrates as referring to a much needed reform in morals, and saying, "You may pass the remainder of your days in sleep, or despair of finding out a sufficient expedient for this purpose; if God, in His providence, do not send you some other instruction." Again, he describes the great philosopher as reproving Alcibiades for going to the temple to pray, on the ground of its uselessness, declaring that he must wait for further light before he could learn how to behave towards gods and towards men; and then in answer to the remark of his pupil, "Who will instruct me, for gladly would I see this man, who he is," the sage replied, "He is one who cares for you; but, as Homer represents Minerva taking away the darkness from the eyes of Diomedes, that he might distinguish a god from a man, so it is necessary that he should first take away the darkness from your mind, and then bring near those things, by which you shall know good and evil." If such are the confessions of the wisest men of antiquity who lived beyond the light of Bible teachings, it will scarcely be controverted that for the uneducated and unthoughtful, a written revelation would be of immense service.

So with regard to the questions of right and wrong, good and evil, which Socrates seems to have acknowledged could be determined only by the coming or incarnation of Deity, even Strauss refers to "the arbitrary manner in which the contemporary sophists confounded all moral notions. To them, according to the maxim of Pythagoras, man was the measure of all things: nothing was naturally good or bad, but only by an arbitrary rule of men, to which the individual need not bind himself, but as the authors of those rules established them for their own advantage, it was open to the individual to call good and put in practice whatever was agreeable or useful to himself. The art of justifying such conduct, argumentatively, of shaking the foundation of all existing principles in religion and morals, of * strengthening the weaker cause,' *i. e.* of making right of wrong, was taught and published by the sophists, but in point of fact all that they did was to put into a methodical form what all the world around them was practising already," (Vol. I. p. 243). That there has been no improvement upon these ancient sophists in recent times, may be inferred from the fact that the most distinguished skeptics, as Lord Bolingbroke and Volney, can discover no obligation to morality outside of self love; that Hobbes finds the sole foundations of right and wrong to exist in the civil law; that Rousseau says "all the morality of our actions lies in the judgment we ourselves form of them "; that the Earl of Shaftesbury declares, "All the obligations to be virtuous arise from the advantages of virtue, and disadvantages of vice"; and that other infidel writers, who refuse to recognize the source, the standard, and the sanction of morality, made known in the Bible, uniformly take ground in relation to this vital subject, which unbelievers themselves can see would speedily lead to the entire overthrow of social order.

III. It will be admitted that if God is the Being described by Deists, as infinitely wise, infinitely powerful, delighting to reveal Himself amid the wonders of the material globe, and amid the still greater wonders of the human heart, too merciful to punish His creatures except by the inexorable operation of nature's laws, there is at least a strong probability that He would make Himself and our duty more fully known by a written revelation, in view of the fact that such a revelation must be an unspeakable blessing to multitudes of the ignorant and weak-minded. Let us concede, for the sake of argument, that a few of the highly-educated, and strong-minded, and scientific, can get along very well without such a revelation; yet they will hardly set themselves up as gods to do the thinking for the rest of the world; and will they have no compassion upon the millions of their fellow-men, who have not been favored with their intellectual vigor and literary advantages? Although these gifted ones need nothing more than the heavens to declare the glory of God, and the firmament to show His handiwork, of which the

Psalmist says, "There is no speech, and there are no words: not at all is their voice heard "(Alexander's Translation), will they not permit the voice of God to be heard in articulate utterance, addressing the poor, the downtrodden, the sorrowing, the toiling, that constitute the vast majority of earth's dying population? If He is the God they represent Him to be, and *could* utter His voice distinctly in the silence or through the discordant notes of nature, so that men may definitely understand Him, He would certainly respond in audible accents to the cry of anguish that comes every moment from many a sinful or stricken soul. If He could utter His voice, and will not, whatever His respect for the stability of nature's laws and for the sufficiency of nature's light, then He is not what they represent Him to be, but a dreadful and unapproachable tyrant, cold and unfeeling as Strauss himself.

IV. It will be admitted that if God has spoken anywhere in a written revelation, it is found in the book commonly called the Bible, or the Sacred Scriptures; for so far as we are concerned, no other book claims to be of supernatural origin. It is taken for granted that no one will meet this statement by reference to the book of Mormon, or the Koran, each of which asserts its supernatural origin, for the argument is addressed only to sensible men; and no sensible man will institute any comparison between these books and the book which challenges our attention, and commands our faith, as the word of God. Both of these books acknowledge the authority of the Bible, and the divine mission of Jesus Christ, asserting for themselves that they contain nothing more than a subsequent revelation from heaven. Those who will take the pains to read them, instead of receiving at second hand what infidels sometimes say in their praise in order to discredit the truth of Christianity, will at once perceive that in many respects they are the plainest plagiarisms from the Scriptures, and that exactly as they depart from the Scriptures to pursue a line of original thinking, they fall to the level of the coarsest superstitions, the lowest errors, and the most brutal vices. It would be an insult to your understanding, therefore, to waste time in proving that they do not deserve serious consideration; but upon the premises already established we may at once proceed to the examination of the book to which they owe whatever merit they possess, and which is emphatically its own witness to its supernatural origin.

First, it presents a code of morals that is altogether unnatural, and hence could not have originated with man. Bruno Bauer, in his "Criticism of the Evangelical Narrative of the Synoptic Gospels," as quoted by

Auberlen, says, "In no section of the Gospels, not even the smallest, are there wanting views which violate, offend, and arouse human nature and feeling "(Divine Revelation, p. 74). Be it so, but it only strengthens the force of the argument that the Gospels did not find their source in human nature and feeling. Did human nature and feeling originate such expressions as these, "Blessed are ye, when men shall revile you, and persecute you, and shall say all manner of evil against you falsely for my sake. . . . Whosoever is angry with his brother without a cause, shall be in danger of the judgment; . . . but whosoever shall say. Thou fool, shall be in danger of hell fire; . . . Ye have heard that it was said by them of old time. Thou shalt not commit adultery: but I say unto you, that whosoever looketh upon a woman to lust after her, hath committed adultery with her already in his heart; . . . I say unto you. Swear not at all, . . . but let your communication be Yea, yea; Nay, nay: for whatsoever is more than these, cometh of evil; . . . Ye have heard that it hath been said. An eye for an eye, and a tooth for a tooth: but I say unto you. That ye resist not evil: but whosoever shall smite thee on thy right cheek, turn to him the other also. And if any man will sue thee at the law, and take away thy coat, let him have thy cloak also. And whosoever shall compel thee to go a mile, go with him twain. Give to him that asketh thee, and from him that would borrow of thee turn not thou away. Ye have heard that it hath been said. Thou shalt love thy neighbor, and hate thine enemy; but I say unto you. Love your enemies, bless them that curse you, do good to them that hate you, and pray for them that deepitefully use you, and persecute you." All these remarkable statements are found in a single chapter of the Gospel by Matthew, and well might Bauer say that they "violate, offend, and arouse human nature and feeling." This is shown by the fact that the traditions of the Elders had added to the teachings of the Pentateuch the clause, "hate thine enemy "; for no such words are found in the Old Testament, but they so fully express human nature and feeling that they were subjoined to the command, "love thy neighbor," as if they formed part of the sacred canon. It is still further shown by the fact that men everywhere recognize the truth of the maxim, "Self-defence is the first law of nature," and scout the precept to turn the cheek to be smitten, because, as they assert, it is against nature. Of course it is against nature, and therefore human nature never suggested such precepts, and never imagined the possibility of a meek and unresisting endurance of evil and of wrong to the very last extremity. But the more unnatural the infidels can show the morality of the Bible to be, the more conclusively they prove the supernatural character and origin of the Bible, since the code it contains could not have sprung from the heart of man.

Second, the way of salvation revealed in the Gospels lifts them entirely above the discovery or invention of human nature, as attested in all ages and in all lands, and even in the experience of every awakened sinner who is led to ask the thrilling question, "What must I do to be saved?" If we look back to ancient times, history tells us how universally men sought to propitiate the favor of the gods by bloody sacrifices, and costly offerings, and self-inflicted tortures. If we look at heathen nations now existing, the same disposition to purchase immunity from punishment and suffering by personal effort and endurance is everywhere manifested. If we look at Christendom during the past eighteen centuries, we see what a constant struggle it has required on the part of comparatively a few faithful witnesses to maintain the testimony of Jesus and the Apostles concerning the absolute freeness of redemption. If we look at each inquirer who is aroused to his urgent need of pardon, and directs his prayer to God for mercy, we discover how deeply implanted in human nature is the thought, that eternal life can be attained only as the result and reward of tears and vows and resolutions and our own righteousness. It is doubtful whether, out of the great multitude of real Christians, who are found amid much that is merely nominal, even one when startled by the Spirit of God in the death-sleep of sin, immediately accepted the assurance of forgiveness through the finished work of Christ, instead of thinking about God with distrust and suspicion and fear, and delaying for at least a little while in order to get better before simply believing. Yet all over the New Testament it is written as if with a sunbeam that the sinner wanting to be saved has nothing to do, because all the doing was done when Jesus bowed His head on the cross and rose again for our justification.

Its language is, "This is my blood of the New Testament, which is shed for many for the remission of sins," (Matt. xxvi. 28), "The Son of man is come to seek and to save that which was lost," (Luke xix. 10); " For God so loved the world, that he gave his only begotten Son, that whosoever believeth in him should not perish, but have everlasting life," (John iii. 16); "He that heareth my word, and believeth on him that sent me hath everlasting life, and shall not come into condemnation [or judgment]; but is passed from death unto life," (John v. 24); "To him give all the prophets witness, that through his name whosoever believeth in him shall receive remission of sins," (Acts x. 43); "By him all that believe are justitied from all things," (Acts xiii.39); "Believe on the Lord Jesus Christ, and thou shalt be saved," (Acts xvi. 31); "To him that worketh not, but believeth on him that justitieth the ungodly, his faith is counted for righteousness," (Rom. iv. 5); "The gift of God is eternal life through Jesus Christ our Lord," (Rom. vi. 23); "There is therefore now no condemnation to them which are in Christ Jesus," (Rom. viii. 1); "Christ hath redeemed us from the curse of the law," (Gal. iii. 13); "Accepted in the beloved; in whom we have redemption through his blood, the forgiveness of sins, according to the riches of his grace," (Eph. i. 6, 7); "But now, in Christ Jesus, ye who sometimes were far off, are made nigh by the blood of Christ," (Eph. ii. 13); "Ye are complete in him," (Col. ii. 10); "Not by works of righteousness which we have done, but according to his mercy he saved us," (Tit. iii. 5); "Wherefore he is able also to save them to the uttermost that come unto God by him, seeing he ever liveth to make intercession for them," (Heb. vii. 25); "Once in the end of the world hath he appeared to put away sin by the sacrifice of himself," (Heb. ix. 26); "Forasmuch as ye know that ye were not redeemed with corruptible things, as silver and gold, ... but with the precious blood of Christ," (1 Pet. i. 18, 19); "The blood of Jesus Christ his Son cleanseth us from all sin," (1 John i. 7); "Thou wast slain, and hast redeemed us to God by thy blood," (Rev. v. 9); "Whosoever will, let him take the water of life freely," (Rev. xxii. 17).

Such is a hurried illustration of the teachings of the entire Bible, that in faultless harmony and perfect unity set forth from Genesis to Revelation the way of salvation through a crucified and risen Christ. That it is a way of salvation which offends and arouses human nature and feeling is obvious, because it has been and still is the most difficult thing in the world to prevent the Church itself from lapsing into apostasy upon the single point of justification by faith alone. A large proportion of Paul's Epistles is occupied with his defence of this fundamental point, showing how hard it was in his day for men to receive a doctrine that uprooted at a stroke all the fancied worthiness of their own performances; and it is just as hard for men to receive it now. Then when received, human nature and feeling are prone to run into the opposite error, and to argue that because we are saved by grace we may live like the world, sitting deaf and dumb at the foot of the cross. Along with this fixed aversion to a truth so humbling to the pride of the heart as salvation for nothing, there is as manifest a recoil from the simplicity of worship enjoined in the New Testament and practiced by its writers. Human nature and feeling are again aroused and offended by the failure to provide for that inherent love of the pomp and pageantry of a gorgeous ritual, which has been exhibited by almost every sect, when the removal of the persecutor's hand, or the increase of numbers and of wealth, gave an opportunity to gratify the innate taste for show. Thus on the one hand legalism, or a slavish bondage to the law for justication, and on the other hand antinomianism, or a contempt for the law of holiness, on the one hand a relish for display in the worship of God to cultivate, it is affirmed, the aesthetic faculty, and on the other hand, a neglect of assembling together, to none of which the New Testament gives the slightest countenance, indicate the strong and settled tendencies of the heart, even against the recognized authority of Jehovah. How then can we account for it that the writers of the Bible did not yield to that which is natural, but steadfastly maintained a position that has been demonstrated by all history to be altogether unnatural? Surely it is not going too far to say that the only reasonable explanation of the fact, and the only rational understanding of their singular attitude, must be reached in the conclusion that their writings q-re supernatural.

Third, the harmony and unity, already mentioned as prevailing with regard to the way of salvation, are found in relation to every other theme common to writers, separated from each other by many centuries, and embracing men of the most dissimilar calling, culture, and rank. Nay, it is only by comparing one with another, and by studying the testimony of one in the light thrown upon it by the teaching of another, that the power and reality of this harmony and unity can be recognized. For example, we see in the opening verse of the Bible, containing the sublime declaration, "In the beginning God created the heaven and earth," that the word "God" is in the plural, without any necessity whatever arising from the structure of the Hebrew language, while it is the subject or nominative of a verb in the singular. In the first chapter, God alone is mentioned apart from any other name or title, while in the second chapter, when man appears upon the scene, the designation is the Lord God. No reason is assigned for what may seem at first unaccountable, but as we advance into the book we learn that there are three persons in the unity of the divine nature, and that the word *Lord* refers to the coming One by whom man is to be redeemed. So again in the second chapter we read that "the Lord God formed man of the dust of the ground, and breathed into his nostrils the breath of life;" but when He formed woman, "the Lord God caused a deep sleep to fall upon Adam and he slept: and he took one of his ribs, and closed up the flesh instead thereof; and the rib, which the Lord God had taken from man, made [or builded] he a woman, and brought her unto the man. And Adam said, This is now bone of my bones, and flesh of my flesh; . . . therefore shall a man leave his father and his mother, and shall cleave unto his wife."

Not a word is said in explanation of the strange scene, but when we read on until we come to Paul's Epistle to the Ephesians, written nearly fifteen hundred years later, we read, "Husbands, love your wives, even as Christ also loved the church, and gave himself for it; that he might sanctify and cleanse it with the washing of water by the word, that he might present it to himself a glorious church, not having spot, or wrinkle, or any such thing; but that it should be holy and without blemish. So ought men to love their wives as their own bodies. For no man ever yet hated his own flesh, but nourisheth and cherisheth it, even as the Lord the church: for we are members of his body, of his flesh, and of his bones. For this cause [because we are members of his body and flesh and bones] shall a man leave his father and mother, and shall be joined unto his wife, and they two shall be one flesh. This is a great mystery: but I speak concerning Christ and the church." Here then at last the mystery of the creation of man and woman in the second chapter of Genesis is cleared up, and we find that the Lord God designed marriage, which is the very basis of society and the State, to be a perpetual illustration, and type, and parable, and reminder, of the eternal and precious union existing between Christ and the Church. There is not a chapter in the Bible that is not linked in some such manner to some other chapter, and indeed to the entire book, constantly exciting the desire of the devout student to unfold to others the beauties that meet his gaze at every step, constantly convincing him that a book so unique and unsearchable is supernatural in its origin, and yet constantly admonishing him of the failure that must attend his effort to communicate the innumerable proofs of its divinity that shine upon every page. The books of Numbers, Leviticus, and even of the Chronicles, that were perhaps once read by the Christian, if read at all, as a perfunctory and profitless service, glow with a new meaning and with a heavenly radiance when brought to the feet of Jesus, who testifies that all the Scriptures bear witness of Himself, (Luke xxiv. 27, 44; John v. 39, 46); for there each writer hastens to cast his crown, and each narrative and song and prophecy does obeisance to the Crucified, only because God's Spirit directs and leads all.

Fourth, the character of God, as portrayed in the Bible, furnishes additional and conclusive evidence that there is nothing in human nature capable of originating such a book. Whether the view it gives of His being and perfections is correct or incorrect, is not now the question. Every one who possesses the slightest acquaintance with the history of mankind will acknowledge that it is a view entirely different from that presented in the various religions of the earth; and this is all that is asserted in the argument. The two prominent facts that arrest our attention in the records of the nations are their polytheism and idolatry, not only among the barbarous and degraded races, but among the most cultivated and refined. Perplexed by the apparent conflicts in the manifestations of the Deity, and confused by the seeming contradictions in the dealings of providence, the uninspired mind could explain the mystery and solve the problem of mortal existence, only on the supposition that there were lords many, and gods many. The heathen saw the sky on one day bright and blue, and the quiet landscape asleep in the sunshine upon the bosom of summer; but on the next day he beheld the heavens black with the wings of the storm, and the beautiful fields wasted by the desolating tread of the hurricane. In the morning he left his little child laughing and playing at the door; but in the evening on his return home he found it writhing in the ruffian grasp of death, and screaming in its agony. He was therefore driven by these diverse and opposing exhibitions of superhuman power to conclude that there were separate and independent intelligences that presided over the affairs of the world, and very soon, in carrying out the law of induction, he installed a nymph in every grove, and a naiad over every stream, until it is said that in elegant Athens there were thirty thousand divinities recognized, and in their despair of reaching the truth, they at length erected an altar to the unknown god.

How was it possible, then, for the Jewish writers, so far behind the Grecian and Roman sophists in learning and philosophy, to make such announcements as the following: "God saw that the wickedness of man was great in the earth, and that every imagination of the thoughts of his heart was only evil continually," (Gen. vi. 5); "I am the Almighty God; walk before me, and be thou perfect," (Gen. xvii. 1); "Thou shalt have no other gods before me. Thou shalt not make unto thee any graven-image, or any likeness of anything that is in heaven above, or that is in the earth beneath, or that is in the water under the earth: thou shalt not bow down thyself to them, nor serve them," (Ex. xx. 3, 4); "Hear, O Israel, the Lord our God is one Lord," (Deut. vi. 4); "Thine, O Lord, is the greatness, and the power, and the glory, and the victory, and the majesty: for all that is in the heaven and in the earth is thine; thine is the kingdom, O Lord; and thou art exalted as head above all," (1 Chron. xxix. 11); "But will God indeed dwell on the earth! Behold the heaven, and heaven of heavens, can not contain thee," (1 Kings viii. 27); "Whither shall I go from thy Spirit"? or whither shall flee from thy presence '? If I ascend up into heaven thou art there; if I make my bed in hell [hades], behold thou art there; if I take the wings of the morning, and dwell in the uttermost parts of the sea; even there shall thy hand lead me, and thy right hand shall hold me, (Ps. cxxxix. 7-10); "Great is our Lord, and of great power: his understanding is infinite," (Ps. cxlvii. 5); "Holy, holy, holy is the Lord of hosts; the whole earth is full of his glory, (Isa. vi. 3); "God is a spirit; and they that worship him must worship him in spirit and in truth," (John iv. 24); "Neither is there any creature that is not manifest in his sight: but all things are naked and opened unto the eyes of him with whom we have to do," (Heb. iv. 13); "Every good gift, and every perfect gift, is from above, and cometh down from the Father of Lights, with whom is no variableness, neither shadow of turning," (James i. 17); "I am Alpha and Omega, the beginning and the ending, saith the Lord, which is, and which was, and which is to come, the Almighty," (Rev.i.8). Hundreds upon hundreds of similar texts could be easily quoted, equal in sublimity and grandeur of conception, in the ascription to God of infinite holiness and power and wisdom and majesty and truth and goodness and mercy and love and immutability and unity; and the question must be answered, how was it, and why was it, that these writers, many of whom were exceedingly illiterate, made any such just and magnificent discoveries of the divine Being? They inform us in the Old Testament that their countrymen century after century exhibited a proneness to idolatry in the face of their expostulations and warnings, that seemed to be innate and unconquerable, and that at last drove them a peeled and scattered people among the nations of the earth. They inform us in the New Testament that the only worship which is acceptable to God is that of the heart; and yet scarcely had the Apostles fallen asleep, before the mystery of iniquity already working in their day, began to lead multitudes of professing Christians into a departure from spiritual service, and into an approximation to the old idolatry, which shows the inveteracy of man's tendency to a religion foreign to the view presented of God from Genesis to Revelation. In what way, then, were the writers of the scriptures led to form a conception of the Deity abundantly proved to be unnatural, because it has never entered the minds of any other men of any age or race, except so far as borrowed from the Bible? Dr. Mozley has well said in his Bampton Lectures, when speaking of the heathen, "The vulgar believed in many gods, the philosopher believed in a Universal Cause; but neither believed in God. The philosopher only regarded the Universal Cause as the spring of the universal machine, which was necessary to the working of all the parts, but was not thereby raised to a separate order of being from them.... Nothing would have astonished him more than, when he had proved in the lecture-hall the existence of a God, to have been told to worship Him. 'Worship whom?' he would have exclaimed. 'Worship what?' 'Worship how?' "In the Bible we have the Universal Cause revealed to us as a living and personal God, clothed with attributes that instantly challenge the homage of the loftiest intelligences, demanding worship in direct opposition to universal polytheism and idolatry; and this fact alone is sufficient to establish the supernatural origin of the Scriptures.

Fifth, suggested by the foregoing view of the character of God, it may be well to notice the catholic spirit that breathes through the Gospels and Epistles, the liberty of conscience they secure, and their utter condemnation of all bigotry, sectarianism, and persecution. It is a common and merited taunt of infidelity that Christians are divided into many and opposing factions, and that the pathway of the Church across the centuries is too often marked by the blood of those who were slain for presuming to differ from the decisions of ecclesiastical authority. Even to-day Turkish soldiers may be seen standing with fixed bayonets in the Church of the Holy Sepulchre at Jerusalem to prevent so-called Christians who worship at the tomb of Jesus from tearing each other to pieces. But all this, humiliating as it is to every true child of God, only shows that strife and hatred and violence are natural to man, and that the book which gives no countenance to such works of the flesh must be supernatural. No attempt is here made to defend what is called Christianity, but only Christ; no effort is put forth to justify the conduct of His professed followers, but only to vindicate the truth of His word. It is impossible for any unprejudiced believer to look abroad over Christendom without grief and shame and pain. Instead of the extorted admiration of the heathen in early times, "Behold, how these Christians love one another," too often it must be said, "Behold, how these Christians hate one another!" Sectarian jealousies, rivalries, and heart-burnings; ministerial pride, ambition, and self seeking; denominational peculiarities permitted to act as a bar to brotherly fellowship; the religious press frequently prostituted to the ignoble purpose of gratifying personal vindictiveness, or of achieving political triumphs; false doctrine, formality, worldliness abounding in the Church; the pulpit in many instances turned into a rostrum for the display of genius and wit to amuse the crowd, and to hide from them the tremendous realities of eternity;—such, it must be confessed with sorrow, is the spectacle that too commonly meets our gaze. But it is a spectacle as foreign to the New Testament as darkness is to light, as sin is to holiness, as the displeasure of God is to His approval; and hence while it fully reveals the natural disposition of the human heart, it also fully reveals the supernatural origin of the Bible that utters a stern and sweeping denunciation of it all.

Sixth, the indirect and manifold blessings conferred by the Bible upon the world at large, far beyond those derived from all other sources combined, form no weak argument to prove that it could not have been the work of men, least of all of men who for the most part were uneducated, who lived in an obscure country, and who wrote at various intervals commencing more than three thousand years ago, and closing their ministry nearly two thousand years ago. Professor Huxley is the last person from whom one would expect a kind word for the Bible, and yet even he writes, "I have always been strongly in favour of secular education, in the sense of education without theology; but I must confess I have been no less seriously perplexed to know by what practical measures the religious feeling, which is the essential basis of conduct, was to be kept up, in the present utterly chaotic state of opinion on these matters, without the Bible. The pagan moralists lack life and color, and even the noble Stoic, Marcus Antoninus, is too high and refined for an ordinary child. Take the Bible as a whole; make the severest deductions which fair criticism can dictate for short-comings and positive errors; eliminate, as a sensible teacher would do, if left to himself, all that it is not desirable for a child to occupy himself with; and there still remains in this old literature a vast residuum of moral beauty and grandeur. And then consider the great historical fact that, for three centuries, this book has been woven into the life of all that is best and noblest in English history; that it has become the national epic of Britain, and is familiar to noble and simple, from John O' Groat's house to Land's End, as Dante and Tasso were once to the Italians; that it is written in the noblest and purest English, and abounds in exquisite beauties of a merely literary form; and finally that it forbids the veriest hind, who never left his village, to be ignorant of the existence of other countries and other civilizations, and of a great past, stretching back to the furthest limits of the oldest nations in the world. By the study of what other book could the children be so humanized, and made to feel that each figure in that vast historical procession fills, like themselves, but a momentary space in the interval between two eternities; and earns the blessings or the curses of all time, according to its effort to do good and hate evil, even as they also are earning their payment for their work?" (Contemporary Review, Dec. 1870).

It is well said that "this book has been woven into the life of all that is best and noblest in English history," and it may be added, in the history of every other nation that has known the unspeakable value of an open Bible. Think of its obvious and acknowledged influence upon the progress of human thought and literature. Think of its relation to civil and religious liberty, yet commanding subjection to the powers that be, and dissociating the Christian from all connection with earthly government, except in enjoining obedience. Think of the benefit it has been to woman, breaking the cruel chains that have bound her as the helpless victim of man's lust and tyranny in all heathen lands, and crowning her with tender respect as the mistress of the home and the affections. Think of the matchless wisdom it exhibits in dealing with the perplexing question of slavery, which was too difficult for the statesmen of the nineteenth century to solve without the battle of the warrior with confused noise, and garments rolled in blood, when it did not seize the institution with violent grasp, but inculcated precepts and taught principles, that could turn every slaveholder into a kind master, and every slave into a freeman, in all but the name, or even into a "brother beloved "of him whom he served. Think of the arrest it lays, as if with the hand of God, upon the wayward impulses of the heart, forbidding with solemn warning of inevitable penalty in this world, and the world to come, the indulgence of vicious, debased and revengeful propensities, that would so manifestly gain the sway but for its mighty check; it is not strange Benjamin Franklin is said to have written to Thomas Paine, when about to publish his Age of Reason, the significant sentence,

"Don't unchain the tiger." Think of the constant and earnest encouragement it gives to the pursuit of "whatsoever things are true, whatsoever things are honest, whatsoever things are just, whatsoever things are pure, whatsoever things are lovely, whatsoever things are of good report; "and then let the sincere inquirer after truth determine whether it is not its own credible witness to its supernatural origin.

Seventh, personal experience of its power furnishes the most conclusive evidence in behalf of its divinity. Nor will it avail the skeptic to reply, as he is continually doing, that the Chinese, the Hindoos, the Mohammedans, the worshippers of a misshapen fetish in Central Africa, and the savages of the Western Continent, can plead the same experience, for a very low degree of intelligence will convince the most careless observer that the experience of a true Christian is no less unique than the book from which it is derived. It is not an experience of mental culture merely, although the obedient student of the Bible is a far abler and wiser man than he would be without it, but it is a moral change as striking and complete as a new birth, as life from the dead. The description given by Paul of certain Christians in Corinth is true of vast numbers in all lands: "Be not deceived: neither fornicators, nor idolaters, nor adulterers, nor effeminate, nor abusers of themselves with mankind, nor thieves, nor covetous, nor drunkards, nor revilers, nor extortioners, shall inherit the kingdom of God. And such were some of you: but ye are washed, but ye are sanctified, but ye are justified in the name of the Lord Jesus, and by the Spirit of our God," (1 Cor. vi. 9-11). Has any other religion ever wrought so marvellous a transformation as this, and is not the book supernatural that can turn through simple faith in its testimony the body, that was a foul cage of unclean birds, into a temple of the Holy Ghost*? Yet multitudes would stand forth, if the opportunity were given, to testify under oath that what was true of the Corinthians, in passing from the slime of vice into cleanness and consecration to Christ, is also true of them. Each would say with the man to whom Jesus gave sight, "One thing I know, that, whereas I was blind, now I see," (John ix. 25). Each would say, "once I perceived no repulsiveness in sin, no attractiveness in holiness, no deformity in myself, no beauty in Christ; but now, God knows, it is my most fervent desire to be entirely conformed to His perfect character, and to be rid at once and forever of all that is selfish and sensual and sinful in thought, word, or deed. I recognize the inherent rightfulness and the absolute necessity of the declaration of the Bible, that without holiness no man shall see the Lord, and I can truthfully affirm that the things I formerly hated I love, and the things I formerly loved I hate with utter hatred." Is such testimony as this, borne by myriads, any one of whom would be believed in any court of the world, to go for nothing, and is such experience as this possible on any other theory than the supernatural origin of the Bible?

Especially is the Christian's experience of value as he advances in years, and discovers more and more clearly the profound acquaintance of the Scriptures with the secret emotions of his heart, and a deeper spiritual meaning in every verse, and always loftier heights of glory above which Christ sits enthroned; and still more is it of value when his warfare is accomplished, and his work on earth is finished. Then while sight and hearing and friends and the world and life are failing, he finds what the Bible is to him with its clear, strong assurance, "The eternal God is thy refuge, and underneath are the everlasting arms," (Deut. xxxiii 27). "Bring me the Book," said Sir Walter Scott | on his dying bed. "What book?" inquired his I son-in-law. "There is but one book," replied the departing novelist, historian, and poet; and the Bible was placed reverently in his hands. Yes, there is but one book whose light pierces the awful darkness of the grave, and guides the weary spirit of the believer home to the bright land, described in language which Robert Burns said he could never read without weeping, where "God shall Wipe away all tears from their eyes; and there shall be no more death, neither sorrow, nor crying, neither shall there be any more pain: for the former things are passed away," (Rev. xxi. 4). Contrast these sweet words with the unutterably sad dedication of Strauss's Life of Jesus to the memory of his dead brother, in which he praises his courage and self-possession in refusing to yield, "under circumstances which might have made the steadiest quail and shaken the strongest faith," to the delusion of seeking comfort in the thought of a future world. Contrast them with the melancholy dedication of Renan's Life of Jesus to the memory of his dead sister, in which he invokes her, like the ancient heathen, as his good genius, beseeching her to reveal truth to him; and then say whether the experience of Paul, "having a desire to depart, and to be with Christ, which is far better," is not infinitely more desirable than the cold speculations or gloomy bravery of infidelity?

Some years ago it was my privilege to meet on the shores of Lake Geneva a young American, who was suffering with spinal disease, that had crippled and pained him from his birth. His pale face, and shrunken limbs, and curved back, gave indication of the agony he had endured, but his soul basked in the sunshine of his Saviour's smile. On one occasion he went for a day's change and recreation to the town of Bex, the terminus at that time of the railroad through the valley, and the place to which many travellers gathered on entering or leaving Italy. He was seated at a table in a large dining room with a number of tourists who had just crossed the Alps, and were waiting for the train, when his attention was called to the loud remarks of a tall, robust, and handsome man; and he soon learned that the remarks were directed with many a shaft of ridicule and wit against the Bible. The skeptic, having finished his dinner, was in the act of withdrawing from the table, when the young American said to him gently, "May I detain you a moment?" ""Certainly," was the kind reply, as the stranger glanced at the sickly youth, not knowing what he wanted. "I only wish," said the Christian, with his weak and plaintive voice, "to tell you briefly my history. I was born in the United States of America, and have always been in my body as you see me now, only worse. My father died in my infancy, and there was no one to love me or care for me but my mother. I had no childhood, but when the boys were playing and shouting in the streets, I was lying in a darkened room, moaning with pain. Under God I owe my life from day to day to the unwearied tenderness and watchfulness of that mother, who thought, when I had struggled on to the age of a young man, that a visit to the holy land, I had so longed to see, would interest me, and might possibly benefit my health. We reached Palestine in safety, but there my mother was suddenly seized with fever, and was laid away in the grave, and now I am on my way home to die too. The only joy left me on earth is the hope of meeting my mother again with Jesus, in heaven; would you take that joy from me?"

"No, no," said the infidel, while the tears ran down his face, "I would not. Keep your hope and your joy, and I crave your pardon for having said a word to wound you." "Oh," exclaimed the Christian, "thank God, you cannot deprive me of my comfort, for I know here," he added, as he placed his hand upon his heart, "how precious is Christ, and how true is His word; but to-day you have poisoned the happiness of some of these young men, who have listened to your cruel harangue against the Bible. You are strong, and do not feel your need of God; but they may come very soon to sorrow and disappointment and temptation and death; and you have done all you can to take away their only shelter and support in the hour of need." The powerful man stood for a moment silent and humbled before the pale youth, and then said solemnly, "I was wrong, and deserve your reproof. Never again will I speak in the presence of others as I did to-day," and respectfully taking the hand of the Christian he withdrew. It may be there are young men now present who have been terribly injured by the jest or sneer of some skeptic; or it may be they are weak enough to imagine that it is a proof of superior intelligence to profess infidel sentiments. But the time is drawing near when the sneer, from which you recoiled as from a real danger, will return to curse you; and the sentiments you admire will be like ghosts in the darkness, that will not down at your bidding. Nay, even now, day by day, they are exerting an influence which can not be otherwise than exceedingly disastrous both to your mental and moral constitution. Men have been great, as the world calls it, in spite of their infidelity, but no one was ever great by reason of his infidelity, while thousands have been truly great by their personal devotion to Jesus. Then when we think of the dangers besetting the soul at every step—who can estimate them? "Wherewithal shall a young man cleanse his way? By taking heed thereto according to thy word," (Ps. cxix. 9).

CHAPTER 7
ALLEGED CONTRADICTIONS

As we enter upon the subject now before us, a remark previously made must be borne in mind concerning the different designs of the four Evangelists in their different narratives. Let us suppose that four men should undertake to write the Life of Napoleon Bonaparte, but conscious of the magnitude of their task, each should assign to himself a special part of the subject, one aiming to present him to the world chiefly as a great soldier, another as a civil ruler promoting the material interests of France, another exhibiting Him as a legislator providing a code of laws for the Empire, and another portraying him in his more private and domestic relations. It is easy to see that each would range over the entire field of his remarkable history, in order to find proofs and illustrations of the particular point in view, without reference, it may be, to the chronological order of events, and without clashing with the purposes of the other writers. It is easy also to perceive that there might be real agreement in their testimony, where a hasty observer would conclude that he could discover innumerable discrepancies and even irreconcilable contradictions,

Hence Archbishop Whately, in his masterly little treatise called "Historic Doubts Relative to Napoleon," and containing an ironical Dedication to Strauss and two other skeptics, takes up the line of argument pursued by the German infidel in his Life of Jesus, that Henry Rogers well says should be entitled, "A collection of all the difficulties and discrepancies which honest criticism has discovered, and perverted ingenuity has imagined, in the four Evangelists;" and he conclusively shows that according to the reasoning Strauss applies to the credibility of the Gospel history, no such man as Napoleon ever existed. We may go further and affirm that by the same mode of reasoning no event of the past, which has been described in all its features by two or more witnesses, can be established; and that no fact of the present, to which two or more witnesses testify in its details, may not be discredited. If, for example, two witnesses were to come into court, one swearing that he saw the prisoner at the bar shoot a man who was standing, the other swearing that he saw the prisoner shoot the same man when the latter was lying on the ground, without stopping to explain that there were two successive shots; or if one witness should make oath that he saw the prisoner inciting a riot, and another witness should make oath that he saw the prisoner in connection with others inciting the rabble to a riot, it is not unfair to say that Strauss would promptly seize upon these discrepancies to prove a contradiction in the testimony.

Perhaps he was led into such a method of treating the narratives of the four Evangelists by the unhappy attempts of many Commentators and Expositors to construct what they are pleased to name "A Harmony of the Gospels." In one sense there is harmony, for there is not the slightest disagreement in the four separate and independent accounts of the life of Jesus; but in another sense it is absurd to suppose that they should always relate the same events, or present them in the same order; for they were written with different thoughts, to speak after the manner of men, controlling the minds of the different authors. Thus every attentive reader of the Gospels must have noticed that it was the design of Matthew to give us a portrait of Jesus in His special relationship to Israel as King of the Jews, without at all observing the order of history, for events are brought together that were separated by the interval of months, and are frequently recorded as if they had occurred before other events which in fact preceded them. A single illustration out of many will make this plain. In Matthew v. vi. and vii. we have the Sermon on the Mount, and in Matthew viii., we find the healing of the leper. But in Mark i. we learn that this miracle was wrought after the healing of Peter's wife's mother, while Matthew reverses the order, and that it preceded the Sermon on the Mount. But why, it may be asked, must we conclude that Mark was more observant than Matthew of the actual order of events? The answer is, because we perceive in Mark such expressions as "immediately," "forthwith," "straightway," "the same day," "the next day," and other notes of time, that are in keeping with his purpose to furnish a picture of the Lord Jesus as the prompt, obedient, and faithful servant, moving with unceasing alacrity to do the Father's bidding, and to manifest the Father's glory.

But did not Matthew know when the events occurred which he relates? Even admitting that he was an obscure Jew writing a narrative for his own amusement, would it not have been a task a child could accomplish to preserve the order of the various scenes and speeches that made up the public life of Jesus? Then when he had published his story, which was soon read by tens of thousands all over the Roman empire, would it not have been easy enough for the other Evangelists to follow, and to shape their accounts to agree precisely with his own"? Either these Evangelists were the most careless and silly men that ever ventured to write a line, and if so we must account for the sublimity of their conceptions, and for the majestic power of their Gospels, that have commanded for eighteen hundred years the homage of the noblest minds of earth, or they had an object to accomplish in departing from the track of each other's statements. Conceding for a moment that at first they wrote different accounts which contained all sorts of legendary traditions, and were full of mistakes, and forced them face to face in fiat contradiction with one another, it is amazing that on the discover of the mistakes and contradictions, men who were embellishing these legendary traditions in part by inventions of their own, did not at once bring their accounts into nearer correspondence. When we discover that they made no attempt to remove the apparent discrepancies that meet the eye of the superficial observer, it is as rational as it is reverent to conclude that the failure to correct what many suppose to be their mistakes, was not owing to human imperfection, but to divine perfection, in their separate histories. It is, therefore, the total spiritual blindness of Strauss, and others like him who undertake to deal with the word of God, to which so many of the alleged contradictions are due; for they can not see the beautiful design of each inspired writer in his own particular narrative of Jesus and the resurrection.

Another source of alleged contradictions is found in the errors that have crept into the manuscripts, occasioned generally by the striking resemblance of several letters in the Hebrew and Greek alphabets, and these errors could not have been avoided except by a perpetual miracle preventing the blunders of thousands of transcribers through hundreds of years. Of course it is known to all that previous to the invention of printing in the fifteenth century, books were produced and perpetuated by the laborious process of copying with the pen, and in such a process mistakes would inevitably occur, unless we suppose that God infallibly inspired a vast multitude of mere copyists, of which the Bible itself contains no hint. Perhaps there is not a printed book in the world of any considerable size that is entirely free from typographical errors, and the most careful copy of the most important manuscript will doubtless exhibit defects of some kind. It was a happy thought, therefore, that suggested to the infidels of Germany and Great Britain, long before the days of Strauss, the propriety of a critical and minute examination of all the Hebrew and Greek manuscripts known to be in existence, with the hope that the various readings which they expected to discover would destroy the credibility of the more recent and popular versions of the Bible. Such was their flourish of trumpets that the devout and learned Bengel, who lived a hundred and fifty years ago, was dismayed, and entered upon the study of all the manuscripts of Europe with intense anxiety. At length, after long and diligent search, he wrote in 1721 to a friend, with a joyful and fully confirmed spirit, "Eat simply the bread of the Scriptures as it presents itself to thee; and do not distress thyself at finding here and there a small particle of sand which the millstone may have left in it. Thou mayst, then, dismiss all those doubts which at one time so horribly tormented myself. If the Holy Scriptures—which have been so often copied, and which have passed so often through the faulty hands of ever-fallible men—were absolutely without variations, the miracle would be so great, that faith in them would no longer be faith. I am astonished, on the contrary, that the result of all those transcriptions has not been a greater number of readings."

The skeptics raised a great shout of triumph when it was understood that critical science had detected 30,000 various readings in the different manuscripts; but, as Cardinal Wiseman says, "In all this mass, although every attainable source has been exhausted; although the fathers of every age have been gleaned for their readings; although the versions of every nation, Arabic, Syriac, Coptic, Armenian, and Ethiopian, have been ransacked for their renderings; although manuscripts of every age from the sixteenth upwards to the third, and of every country, have been again and again visited by industrious swarms to rifle them of their treasures; although, having exhausted the stores of the West, critics have travelled like naturalists into distant lands to discover new specimens—have visited, like Scholz, or Sebastiani, the recesses of Mount Athos, or the unexplored libraries of the Egyptian and Syrian deserts—yet has nothing been discovered, no, not one single various reading, which can throw doubt upon any passage before considered certain or decisive in favor of any important doctrine These various readings, almost without an exception, leave untouched the essential parts of any sentence, and only interfere with points of secondary importance, the insertion or omission of an article or conjunction, the more accurate grammatical construction, or the forms rather than the substance of words," (Science and Revealed Religion, Vol. II, pp. 165-6). The result of the conflict so boldly and confidently commenced by the skeptics Michaelis sums up as follows: "They have ceased henceforth to look for anything from those critical researches which they at first so warmly recommended, because they expected discoveries from them that have never been made." This result has been more and more conclusively demonstrated by the more recent investigations of Tregelles, Tischendorf, and other critics, leading us to conclude with Gaussen, "that not only was the Scripture inspired on the day when God caused it to be written, but that we possess this word inspired eighteen hundred years ago; and that we may still, while holding our sacred text in one hand, and in the other all the readings collected by the learned in seven hundred manuscripts, exclaim with thankfulness, I hold in my hands my Father's testament, the eternal word of my God," (The Bible, p. 197).

Another source of the alleged contradictions in the Bible may be traced to a difference in the dates, to which the assertions that are supposed to clash respectively belong, as when it is said at the dawn of creation, "God saw everything that he had made, and, behold, it was very good," (Gen. i. 31); and when it is said fifteen hundred years later, "God saw that the wickedness of man was great in the earth, and that every imagination of the thoughts of his heart was only evil continually," (Gen. vi. 5). Or they may be traced to different modes of reckoning time, as both the Jewish and Roman method are mentioned in the New Testament, and as we find even in English history that, according to what is called "Old Style," Washington was born February 11, 1732, or according to the "New Style," he was born February 22; but every one can see that there is no contradiction. Or they may be traced to the different positions occupied by the sacred writers with reference to the subject treated or the statement made, as when God is said to repent, and not to repent; as when it is declared that the children of God fear Him, and fear Him not; as when Paul teaches that we are justified by faith alone before God, and James teaches that we are justified by works also before men; as when it is still said in every-day language, "man is mortal," and "man is immortal," both being true. Or they may be traced to the different, and sometimes opposite, meaning of the same word, not only in Hebrew and Greek, but in English, as the word "let "signifies both *to permit* and *to hinder*, and the word "prevent "signifies both *to go before or precede, and to obstruct or impede*. Or they may be traced to mistranslations of the original language, which it is the province of accurate scholarship to correct.

Without any further remarks in regard to the origin of alleged contradictions, enough probably has been said to show a thoughtful "and honest inquirer after truth that there are several considerations which should be carefully weighed before he can wisely determine to find real contradictions in the Bible; and it may be well for him to know that neither can infidelity bring forward anything new along this line of attack, nor can it allege a single contradiction that has not been triumphantly answered again and again. Several years ago, immediately after the appearance of Colenso's book on the Pentateuch, a very intelligent and sincere Christian in this city came in deep distress to a Minister of the Gospel, because as it seemed to him, Colenso had conclusively proved a contradiction in two statements of the Bible about the number of Jacob's descendants that went down into Egypt. The reply was, "I have not seen Colenso's book, but bring it to me tomorrow, and you will see that the charge he has urged against God's word, whatever it is, has long since been met and refuted by some Christian writer, who will be summoned to testify the moment you let me know definitely what the infidel Bishop asserts." The next day he came, and after reading Colenso's statement, the Minister took from his library a work by Hengstenberg on the "Genuineness of the Pentateuch," and in a few minutes showed precisely the same argument, and so thorough an exposure of its fallacy, that the gentleman quietly placed Colenso's book in the fire, and turned away with an expression of regret that he had suffered himself to be disturbed for a moment. Let us see whether all of the alleged contradictions of any importance mentioned by Strauss may not be as easily explained.

I. We commence with the two genealogies of Jesus given in Matthew and Luke, which Strauss discusses at some length in the beginning of his second volume, pp. 7-19. A very early explanation of the apparent difficulty asserts that the mother of Joseph, the husband of Mary, married two husbands, and that the two genealogies in the two Gospels are the genealogies of these two husbands, Joseph being the son by birth of one, and the son by adoption of the other. But the true explanation, and the one that is in beautiful accord with the different purposes of the two Evangelists, is found in the fact that Matthew gives us the genealogy of Joseph, while Luke gives us that of Mary. It will be observed that the former goes no further back in the genealogy of Jesus than to prove that He was the son of David, the son of Abraham; but Luke continues the line of His ancestry until he reaches Adam, which was of God. The reason for this is obvious. Matthew wrote for the Jew, and to the Jew it was of necessity that Jesus should be the heir, according to the law, of Joseph, who was descended from the royal branch of David's house, of which two lines had come down unbroken to those days; the line of Solomon, and the line of Nathan. If the genealogy of Mary had been given in Matthew without her connection with her husband, no Jew would have recognized the legal right of Jesus to the throne of David, and at once His claim as the Messiah would have been set aside. The Messiah must be born, not merely of a virgin, not only of a virgin daughter of David, but of one legally united, *i. e.*, in the eye of the law, to a lineal descendant, as Joseph was, of the once reigning house of God. But if Joseph had been His real father, it is plain that He could not have been the Saviour; so that in the opening chapter of the New Testament we behold a miracle of divine wisdom in making Him legally the son of Joseph, which was necessary to establish His right to reign, really the son of Mary, which was necessary to His humanity, and in His divine nature the Son of God, which was necessary to our salvation.

Strauss imputes a mistake to Matthew for omitting certain generations from his table, and yet it is a mistake which no school boy of ordinary intelligence could have committed, for even a school boy with the Old Testament before him could copy the list of names and generations found in Genesis, Numbers, Chronicles, and elsewhere. Why did not the German skeptic also find fault with Ezra for omitting seven generations in giving his personal genealogy, and no one will deny that he knew his own descent? The truth is the omissions furnish evidence again of divine wisdom, for it is the seed of the wicked Athaliah Matthew drops from his genealogy, while the Gentile Rahab and Ruth are brought in, just to intimate the tender grace which was to be exhibited to the despised and outcast, in the mission and ministry of Jesus. But as one of these two Gospels was written and published before the other, can not every one see that it would have been a very simple thing for the later Evangelist to copy the genealogy of the former, and is it not certain that he would have done so, if there had not been some special reason for the variation? Let skeptics learn to treat the writers of the Bible with the fairness they show to any other class of authors, and most of their alleged contradictions will instantly disappear. Leaving entirely out of view the guiding hand of the Holy Ghost, we can perceive that it served the purpose of Matthew, in presenting Jesus as the son of David, to trace His lineage back from His reputed and legal father, through the royal line of Solomon; and it served the purpose of Luke, in presenting Jesus as the Son of man, to trace Him back from Mary, by whom He became the Son of man, through the royal line of Nathan, but beyond David, beyond Abraham, beyond Adam, up to God. The correctness of the view here given of the two genealogies is verified by the fact which Lightfoot mentions, that the Jewish Rabbinical writers speak contemptuously of Mary as the daughter of Heli, whom Luke also names; and hence there is no contradiction whatever in the accounts.

II. Perhaps the next contradiction most commonly alleged relates to the death of Judas, of whom Matthew states that he "went and hanged himself," (Matt, xxvii. 5); and Peter states that "falling headlong, he burst asunder in the midst, and all his bowels gushed out," (Acts i. 18). It is needless to say that the two statements do not contradict each other, unless it can be shown either that Matthew asserts Judas did not fall headlong, or that Peter asserts he did not hang himself. Matthew does not deny that Judas, after hanging himself, fell headlong; nor does Peter deny that he hanged himself before falling headlong. Only a short time since the daily papers contained an account of a young man who left this city for Chicago, and there securing' a room in one of the magnificent Hotels, proceeded to commit suicide it is said, by poison, stabbing, hanging, and if these methods had failed he had made arrangements to fulfill his desperate purpose by falling into the bathtub that he might be drowned. A little while before a man committed a double suicide somewhere in Indiana, partly by poison, it is asserted, and partly by an artfully contrived guillotine; and yet no one thought of alleging a contradiction in the narratives that were published of these events. Why can not the infidel deal with the Bible as with any other written testimony, and admit that Judas might have first hanged himself upon the edge of one of the rocky precipices or terraces abounding near Jerusalem, and then owing to the breaking of the cord, or the decomposition of his body, have fallen headlong upon the sharp stones beneath that would have crushed and mangled the corpse? Surely any fair-minded skeptic must see in the two statements, not an irreconcilable contradiction, but positive proof of the independence of the two writers, of the absence of all collusion in their narratives, and of their entire freedom from any attempt to make up the Gospel history by inventions of their own.

III. Matthew says that as Jesus departed from Jericho, two blind men who were sitting by the wayside received their sight in answer to their earnest cry, "Have mercy on us, O Lord, thou son of David," (Matt. xx. 30). Mark says that Jesus was going out of Jericho, but speaks of only one blind man, Bartimeus, the son of Timæus, who sat by the highway side, begging, (Mark x. 46). Luke speaks of but one blind man, and says as Jesus was come nigh unto Jericho, the miracle was wrought, (Luke xviii. 35). But observe that he is the only one of the three writers who records the question of the blind man, "Hearing the multitude pass by, he asked what it meant." This question he may have asked as Jesus was entering the city, and learning that the gracious and mighty miracle worker was very near, he may have gone with his companion in blindness and beggary into the city, and waited with the crowd outside the house of Zaccheus until the Messiah appeared, and still followed him with the prayer that was heard and answered. Thus the more carefully the Gospel narratives are scanned, the more clearly- does their perfect consistency appear, and the more certainly are we convinced that in their unstudied simplicity and harmony, they can be traced neither to imposture nor to fanaticism as their source. Or if this explanation, just given of the separate accounts in the three gospels, is rejected as unsatisfactory, there is still another in the fact that the Greek word rendered *come nigh* in Luke does not necessarily imply more than that He *was* nigh or near the city, without determining whether he was entering it, or departing from it, at the time of the occurrence related. No intelligent critic will insist that there is a contradiction, because Matthew mentions two blind men, and Mark and Luke speak of but one; for the latter do not say that there was only one, and it served their purpose best to call special attention to the one who was most prominent, while Matthew briefly and incidentally alludes to the two.

IV. "Then was fulfilled that which was spoken by Jeremy the prophet, saying. And they took the thirty pieces of silver, the price of him that was valued, whom they of the children of Israel did value; and gave them for the potter's field, as the Lord appointed me," (Matt, xxvii. 9, 10). No such words are found in Jeremiah, but in Zechariah we read, "I said unto them, If ye think good, give me my price; and if not, forbear. So they weighed for my price thirty pieces of silver. And the Lord said unto me, Cast it unto the potter: a goodly price that I was prized at of them. And I took the thirty pieces of silver, and cast them to the potter in the house of the Lord," (Zech. xi. 12, 13). Here, it is confidently alleged, there is a plain contradiction; but apart from the fact that some of the most ancient versions, as the Syriac-Peshito, and Persian, and some of the early MSS., omit the word *Jeremiah*; apart from the fact that the Jews regarded Jeremiah as the first of the prophets, in a manner including Zechariah, who quotes him more than once; there is nothing forced or unnatural in supposing that Jeremiah had spoken the words, afterwards recorded by Zechariah. Thus Paul tells the Ephesian Elders "to remember the words of the Lord Jesus, how he said, It is more blessed to give than to receive," (Acts xx. 35), although these words are nowhere recorded in the four Gospels. So Jude informs us of the words of Enoch, the seventh from Adam, who said, "Behold, the Lord cometh with ten thousands of his saints," (Jude 14), though none of the sayings of Enoch are preserved in the Old Testament. Besides all this, some eminent scholars have thought that the 9th, 10th, and 11th chapters of Zechariah were written originally by Jeremiah; and hence in any view there is no contradiction proved. It would be becoming modesty in those who read the Bible to sit with reverent silence in the presence of a difficulty and wait for further light, rather than cavil where so much is divine and precious.

V. Strauss insists that the two accounts contained in Matt. ii. and Luke ii. of the order of events connected with the infancy of Jesus are incompatible, because Matthew says nothing of the residence at Nazareth previous to the nativity, nor of the circumstances which led Joseph and Mary to Bethlehem, nor of the scenes that transpired in the temple; while Luke says nothing of the visit of the wise men from the East, nor of the slaughter of the young children by Herod, nor of the flight to Egypt. But surely no proof of a contradiction can be furnished by the silence of an author concerning transactions which did not fall within his purpose to narrate, for if this rule of criticism should be established, no series of events that have engaged the attention of two or more historians can be believed. There is no reason whatever for not supposing that Joseph and Mary came from Nazareth to Bethlehem; that there Jesus was born; that within the course of a few days afterwards He was presented according to the law in the temple for circumcision; that then the wise men came on their journey; and this led to the escape of Joseph and Mary from the cruelty of Herod. Nor is there any difficulty in supposing that immediately after the infant Jesus was presented in the temple they returned to Nazareth, and subsequently came back to Bethlehem, from which they lied into Egypt, or that they visited the spot, forever so hallowed in their memory and thoughts, during some one of the great annual festivals. Either supposition can be adopted without the slightest strain, and either is infinitely more natural than the theory that the two writers are in conflict with each other, when it would have been so easy for one to copy from the other. But while the separate accounts show that they have given us independent narratives, the omissions of neither show the least contradiction.

VI. Strauss also alludes to the mistake which he thinks Luke commits in the statement, "This taxing was first made when Cyrenius was governor of Syria," (Luke ii. 2). According to Josephus this Cyrenius was not sent to govern the province until at least ten or eleven years after the birth of Jesus, and hence it is taken for granted that Luke is flatly contradicted by history. But why, it may be asked, are we compelled to believe Josephus rather than Luke? What reason is there for assuming that if one of the writers of the Bible and a Jewish or heathen author come into conflict, the former is manifestly wrong, and the latter is plainly right! Does critical science imagine that all writers except Bible writers are inspired to be correct, and that only those who give us the Scriptures are uninspired? But in the instance now before us there is no need to infer that either Josephus or Luke is in error. The clause to which Strauss objects is a parenthesis, and its literal translation, which he must have known, is as follows: "The first census itself was effected while Cyrenius was governor of Syria." In other words, having stated that a decree had gone forth from Caesar Augustus that a general tax should be levied, he then wishes it to be known by the verse in the parenthesis, that this decree must not be confounded with the census itself, which was effected under Cyrenius. Or the word *first* may be rendered, as it is sometimes, "prior to," "*before*," and the sense would then be, this taxing was before that made under Cyrenius. Or it may be that there were two taxings, in both of which Cyrenius was concerned, for it is a remarkable fact that Justin Martyr, who lived not very long after Luke, asserts three times that Jesus was born under Cyrenius, and the heathen writers of that time did not deny the truth of the statement. Certainly no one who is familiar with the gospel of Luke, and with the Acts of the Apostles, of which also he was the author, can think that he would fall into such an inexcusable blunder, that might have been avoided by the most stupid rustic who lived at that day; and certainly it seems more charitable and more honest to conclude that he knew what he was saying in the narratives, than to hurry to the supposition that a mistake has been found in the Bible.

VII. According to the three first Evangelists Jesus was nailed to the cross at the third hour of the day, that is to say, at nine o'clock in the morning; the sun was darkened at the sixth hour, or noon; and He bowed His head in death at the ninth hour, or three o'clock in the afternoon; but according to John the execution did not commence until the sixth hour, or noon. But let us suppose that John, writing in Asia Minor, used the Roman mode of reckoning time, from midnight, so that the sixth hour would be six o'clock in the morning, and the interval between that hour and nine o'clock would be occupied by the necessary preparations, thus bringing the writers into perfect agreement. Or let us remember that in the Greek MSS. numbers are generally expressed by the letters of the alphabet, and that the two Greek letters which stand for 3 and 6 are strikingly alike; and again they can be brought into agreement by seeing that careless copyists have substituted 6 for 3 in the Gospel of John. This too is just precisely what some of the most distinguished scholars claim, and hence they insist that the proper reading in John is the third hour, as with the other Evangelists. But even if both explanations are judged to be unsatisfactory, it is still possible that the three synoptical Evangelists only meant by the third hour that it was past, using an indefinite expression. and that John only meant by the sixth hour that it was approaching, he too using an indefinite expression. At all events it is easier to accept either explanation than to suppose that four men, three of whom had the writings of the first before them, could fall into so meaningless and useless a blunder concerning the hour of the day when the most stupendous fact of human history occurred. We can at least give these writers credit for possessing common sense.

VIII. According to John the risen Jesus, on His appearance to Mary

Magdalene, would not permit her to touch Him, because, He says, "I am not yet ascended to my Father: but go to my brethren, and say unto them, I ascend unto my Father, and your Father; and to my God, and your God," (John XX. 17). According to Matthew, as Mary Magdalene and the other Mary ran to tell the disciples of His resurrection, He met them with a glad recognition; "and they came and held Him by the feet, and worshipped Him," (Matt, xxviii. 9). Here, in order to prove a contradiction, it is assumed that Jesus did not ascend to the Father until the expiration of forty days; but for this view, commonly held even by Christians, there is not the slightest Scriptural authority. His ascension has a two-fold relation, first to His own people, and then to the world at large; for He has entered into heaven, "now to appear in the presence of God for us," (Heb. ix. 24); and He is also "the head over all things to the church," (Eph. i. 22). In like manner on the day of His resurrection He appeared to the disciples, and breathed on them, saying, "Receive ye the Holy Ghost," (John xx. 22), and they did then and there receive Him as the power of an endless life; but on the day of Pentecost the Holy Ghost descended in visible pomp and majesty, as the power of testimony and service, (Acts ii). It was appropriate, therefore, that He should not permit the touch of a human hand before ascending to the Father, for He must fulfill the type of the high priest entering into the holy place on the great day of atonement, when no man could be in the tabernacle, (Lev. xvi. 17); but having ascended, He hastened back, as it were, to satisfy the longing of Mary's anxious and happy heart with the welcoming shout, "All hail!" Forty days later He ascended visibly from the midst of His followers, while His hands were uplifted in priestly benediction to bless them; but it is ignorance of Scripture that leads any to suppose He had not previously ascended, and therefore it is ignorance of Scripture that leads any to suppose there is a contradiction in the two accounts.

Precisely the same remark must be made about the contradiction which Strauss alleges with regard to the second coming of the Lord. "On one occasion Jesus says to His disciples that the Son of Man will return before they shall have completed their Messianic preaching in all the cities of Israel, (Matt. x. 23); another time he says that the second Advent will not occur until the Gospel has been preached in the whole world among all peoples, (Matt. xxiv. 14). Now these are two very different things; Jesus, therefore, must have changed His views very much between the first of these prophecies and the second, or rather it is clear that the one was put into the mouth of Jesus at a time when, and in a circle in which, the kingdom of the Messiah was considered limited to the people of Israel, and the other from a point of view to which the calling of the heathen into that kingdom was already a settled thing," (Vol. I, p. 326). Here again we find utter ignorance of Scripture, that all through the Old and New Testaments teaches the two-fold relation of the second Advent, first to the Jews as an earthly people to be restored to their laud, and second to the Christians of the present dispensation as an heavenly people to be associated with the millennial reign of Jesus over the earth. Think for a moment of a horizontal line representing the Jew, suddenly broken by a circle representing the church, when no note is taken of time, and on the opposite side of the circle the horizontal line commencing again, and you will readily understand these double allusions to the second coming of Christ. So far from finding contradictions, we discover divine wisdom in perfection, tracing that coming in connection with Israel, and then in connection with the Gentile world, and presenting the teachings of Jesus in beautiful harmony. So may all the alleged contradictions which Strauss mentions be easily explained; and as there is no time to consider others, the challenge is here respectfully made to any infidel to show one real contradiction in the Bible from first to last.

IX. None of the alleged contradictions of the Old Testament have been noticed, partly for want of time, and partly because it was thought best to confine attention to the most prominent of those which Strauss imagined he had found in the Gospel history. But there is the less need of turning aside to glance at the Old Testament narratives, because Jesus set the seal of His own divine sanction upon the canon of the Old Testament as a whole, precisely in the form in which we possess it today, and especially upon those portions at which infidelity has always delighted to cavil. Thus He expressly recognizes the truth of the story connected with a universal deluge, (Matt. xxiv. 38, 39; Luke xvii. 27); the truth of the story connected with the destruction of Sodom and Gomorrah, (Matt. xi. 23, 24; Luke xvii. 28, 29); the truth of the story connected with Jonah, (Matt. xii. 39-41); and the truth of the story connected with Lot's wife, (Luke xvii. 32). It is as if He confronted proud man with the solemn words. It is at thy peril if thou believest not these Scriptures, for if thou believest them not thou believest Me not; "and he that believeth not the Son shall not see life; but the wrath of God abideth on him," (John iii. 36). So the Holy Ghost, or, if this expression is offensive to you, the Apostles Peter and Jude and John vouch for the correctness of the narratives concerning the angels that sinned, the flood, the overthrow of Sodom and Gomorrah, and Balaam, (2 Pet. ii. iii.; Jude 6-11; Rev. ii. 14); and in many other places the Old and the New Testaments are so linked together, that it is impossible to deny the credibility of the former without sweeping the latter out of existence. The Bible comes to us, not to discuss scientific questions from the exceedingly narrow standpoint of feeble human reason and limited human knowledge, but with authority it commands our faith. The only time God condescends to argue is when He approaches the lost sinner with the gentle invitation, "Come now, and let us reason together saith the Lord: Though your sins be as scarlet, they shall be as white as snow; though they be red like crimson, they shall be as wool," (Isa. i. 18).

X. Neither does it come within the purpose of these lectures to consider the alleged contradictions between the Scriptures and the discoveries of Science; but it is sufficient to say that if it has been proved, or if it can be proved, that the Scriptures contain the word of God, it is impossible to discover a contradiction between their testimony and true Science? There are many who will obtain a little smattering of science by reading one or two books, or by glancing at the Reviews, and then swell with a conceit of their vast erudition, when, perhaps, the next discovery will prick them like a bag of wind. Darwin, Huxley, Tyndall, and such men, may amuse themselves and the world with their theories as much as they please; and it is possible that in the course of time they may reach some result that will be of real value; but the moment they bring their new-fledged theories to contradict the Bible, that has stood the assaults and storms of four thousand years, their science is no longer science, but audacity and impertinence. Their speculations about God, and eternity, and the soul, and prayer, are of no more consequence than the prattling of infancy or the babbling of idiocy, simply because such subjects do not belong to their department of investigation. Human science, if worthy of the name, moves in an orbit of its own, divine revelation moves in another and distinct orbit, both wheeling around the throne of the Eternal without clashing, and vieing with each other in offering a tribute of praise to Him who made the universe, but no less surely made the Holy Scriptures. If science departs from its proper sphere to meddle with revelation, it will certainly have abundant reason sooner or later to deplore its folly and presumption, as inevitable defeat awaits it from the encounter; and if men were not what they are, they would be on their guard against the rash surmises of the scientists; for the pathway of history for the last fifty years is strewn with the fragments of discarded and despised theories that were once most confidently and tenaciously held.

It is said that when Julian the Apostate was summoning the philosophy, and marshalling the military resources of the Roman empire, to crush Christianity, the distinguished divine, Athanasius, calmly remarked to some of his desponding friends, "It is a little cloud; it will pass away." Tradition relates that not long after, when Julian was mortally wounded in battle, he caught the blood Streaming from his breast, and threw it into the air with the cry, "O Galilean, thou hast conquered." Of course Gibbon dismisses the tradition with contempt, but he writes as follows of the closing scene in the life of one whom he greatly admired: "Whenever he closed his eyes in short and interrupted slumbers, his mind was agitated with painful anxiety; nor can it be thought surprising, that the Genius of the empire should once more appear before him, covering with a funeral veil his head, and his horn of abundance, and slowly retiring from the Imperial tent. The monarch started from his couch, and stepping forth to refresh his wearied spirits with the coolness of the midnight air, he beheld a fiery meteor, which shot athwart the sky, and suddenly vanished. Julian was convinced that he had seen the menacing countenance of the god of war;" and his heathen priests having in vain endeavored to dissuade him from exposing himself in battle, when pierced by the fatal javelin, according to Gibbon he exclaimed, "I die without remorse, as I have lived without guilt. I am pleased to reflect on the innocence of my private life; and I can affirm with confidence, that the supreme authority, that emanation of the Divine Power, has been preserved in my hands pure and immaculate," (Milman's Gibbon's Rome, Vol. II. pp. 499, 501). If he really delivered this false and foolish speech, truly the Galilean had conquered; as the Emperor was left to exhibit the utter deceitfulness of the human heart, and the pitiful vanity and weakness of human nature, even amid the solemnities of death; for no man in his senses believes he spoke the truth. Athanasius was right; it was a little cloud, and soon passed away.

So it may be confidently said of the work that has demanded and received our attention during the last few weeks. It engaged the energies of a far more than ordinary intellect for a period of more than thirty years; but after all "it is a little cloud; it will soon pass away." The writings of the heathen and infidel and heretical assailants of Jesus during the first centuries have long since perished, except as they have been partially preserved in quotations by those who wrote in His defence. The writings of the Deists who infested England in the early part of the 18th century have perished. The writings of the French Philosophers of the same time, after starting into action the hellish forces that did bloody work at the close of the century, have perished. Renan's Life of Jesus ran a brief career, and then perished. Thus must it be with Strauss's Life of Jesus, which has ignominiously failed to accomplish its object, like the assaults of those who preceded him in their attempts to destroy "the word of God, which liveth and abideth forever. For all flesh is as grass, and all the glory of man as the flower. The grass withereth, and the flower thereof falleth away: but the word of the Lord endureth forever," (1 Pet. 1. 23-25). Jesus has said, in language that would be the height of blasphemy, if He were not divine, "Heaven and earth shall pass away, but my words shall not pass away," (Matt. xxiv. 35). Yea, though the world, under the tuition of a Christless culture and a Godless science, is rapidly educated for submission to the Antichrist; though the great mass of the professing Church, faithless to the principles and practices of the New Testament, is soon to be spued out of the mouth of our insulted Lord; Jesus still lives, and His words, that are meeting with a precise fulfillment day by day, still live. "The kings of the earth set themselves, and the rulers take counsel together, against the Lord, and against his anointed, saying. Let us break their bands asunder, and cast away their cords from us. He that sitteth in the heavens shall laugh f the Lord shall have them in derision," (Ps. ii. 2-4).

If the Christian finds himself ready to despond, as He witnesses the astounding spread of infidelity, not only outside but inside the Church, let him remember that Jesus was "declared to be the Son of God with power, according to the Spirit of holiness, by the resurrection from the dead," (Rom. i. 4). Let him turn his anxious thoughts to the working of God's mighty power, "which he wrought in Christ, when he raised him from the dead, and set him at his own right hand in the heavenlies, far above all principality, and power, and might, and dominion, and every name that is named, not only in this world, but also in that which is to come; and hath put all things under his feet, and gave him to be head over all things to the church, which is his body, the fulness of him that filleth all in all," (Eph. i. 20-23). The Church—by which is not meant any particular sect, nor the various denominations together, all of which may go to pieces, by which is not meant those who have a name to live, and are dead, those possessing a form of godliness, and denying the power thereof, but those who are born again, those who are united by the Holy Ghost to the risen Jesus, those who have salvation through faith in His name—the Church is as safe as if already seated by His side upon His throne. "My sheep hear my voice," He says, "and I know them, and they follow me: and I give unto them eternal life; and they shall never perish, neither shall any pluck them out of my hand. My Father, which gave them me, is greater than all; and no one is able to pluck them out of my Father's hand. I and my Father are one," (John X. 27-30). Even in the last days when perilous times shall come, and when the inspired Apostle saw everything in ruins, he adds the cheering assurance, "Nevertheless the foundation of God standeth sure, having this seal, The Lord knoweth them that are his. And, Let every one that nameth the name of Christ depart from iniquity," (2 Tim. ii. 19). Only forget the darkness in looking for the Morning Star that is to usher in His glorious appearing, and nothing can disturb your peace. Blessed be His name, it is for Himself believers who know the truth now watch and wait, without any expectation of the triumph of the church, except as achieved by His visible and personal presence; without any desire to behold the bride reigning on the earth before the coming and coronation of the Bridegroom. Just as heaven would be no heaven but for the sight of Jesus, so the millennium would be no millennium unless He presided in manifested glory over the holy and happy scene. Let skeptical criticism proceed then even to greater lengths than Strauss in its ruthless and ungenerous treatment of His precious word; let skeptical science drift farther and farther away from the written revelation, until the very being of God is denied; let the scoffers of the last days walk after their own lusts, and say with a sneer, "Where is the promise of His coming? for since the fathers fell asleep, all things continue as they were from the beginning of the creation," (2 Pet. iii. 4); "when these things begin to come to pass, then look up, and lift up your heads, for your redemption draweth nigh," (Luke xxi. 28). But the redemption of body as well as soul that draweth nigh for believers is but the signal of a time when "the kings of the earth, and the great men, and the rich men, and the chief captains, and the mighty men, and every bondman, and every freeman, hid themselves in the dens and in the rocks of the mountains; and said to the mountains and rocks, Fall upon us, and hide us from the face of Him that sitteth on the throne, and from the wrath of the Lamb: for the great day of His wrath has come, and who shall be able to stand?" (Rev. vi. 15-17). The coming of Christ will flash the light of truth upon all the paltry excuses of unbelievers, and in that light they will refrain from saying as they now do, "we *could* not believe," but will confess with inexpressible terror, "we *would* not believe." He who is the truth itself has declared, "This is the condemnation, that light is come into the world, and men loved darkness rather than light, because their deeds were evil;" "and ye WILL not come to me, that ye might have life," (John iii. 19; v. 40).

Just because infidelity has its seat not in the head, but in the heart, all attempts to convert the skeptic by argument must necessarily fail, and in the face of the most complete demonstration he illustrates the familiar couplet,

> "He that complies against his will
> Is of his own opinion still."

Men do not want to believe the Bible, because the mind of the flesh is enmity against God, because it lays an arrest upon appetites and passions which they love to gratify, because it utters the stern admonition of a reckoning in the future world for the sins of the present, because it humbles them into the dust by casting the highest not less certainly than the lowest, the most cultivated and refined not less surely than the most ignorant and degraded, upon the grace of God and the atoning sacrifice of Christ for salvation. But let a word of the humblest and poorest, winged by the Holy Ghost, reach the heart, and instantly all objections are answered, all the barriers which unbelief has reared around the soul are swept away, and the proof that the Scriptures are divine shines from every page, like the splendor of the eternal throne. Several years ago a prominent minister of the gospel in Cincinnati delivered a series of carefully prepared discourses on the Evidences of Christianity. Among his hearers were two persons unlike in every respect. One was a highly educated man, the president of an infidel club, who had been commissioned to attend the lectures, and take notes that were subsequently presented for discussion at the meetings of the skeptics; and the other was an old and illiterate colored woman, who attended, not because she understood the arguments, but because she delighted to be where the name of her Saviour was honored. On a certain evening during service, a sleet fell, covering the stone steps of the church building, and as the old woman was leaving at the close of the sermon, she slipped, and might have been severely injured if the infidel, who was descending the steps at the same time, had not caught her and kindly assisted her to the sidewalk. She thanked him, and then said in a low, tremulous voice, "Young master, do you love Jesus"; They parted, but that voice followed him to his room, and started a mighty tide of emotion in his proud heart, and never left him until he had bowed in faith and with tears of adoring gratitude beneath the cross he had despised. The minister hearing that an infidel, who had attended his lectures, was converted, sought his acquaintance, and desired to know what argument had convinced him of his error. "Oh," he replied, "I listened to all of your arguments with unmoved indifference, save when they excited a feeling of intense opposition to the views you advanced: but it was the simple question of an old negro woman, 'do you love Jesus?' that led me to see the cruelty of my conduct towards my best Friend."

Dear, dying hearers, if the poor arguments to which you have listened for several weeks past, so far below the importance of the great subject, have failed to convince any of you who are skeptical that the Bible is the work of God, at least permit me to ask you the searching question, "Do you love Jesus?" If not, why do you not love Him? Has He ever harmed you, or has He ever harmed the world? As Pilate said to the rabble clamoring for His crucifixion, "Why, what evil hath he done?" Would you crucify Him again? Would you grieve His heart, so noble, so good, so loving, by turning away with contemptuous unconcern from His entreating voice? You may forget Him for a time, but you can not always despise His claims upon your confidence and affection. If you continue to neglect Him to the close of your brief mortal existence, God will assuredly shut you up in hell; for He will not permit you to count the blood of His Son a common thing. Other questions may engage your attention now, but sooner or later the question that must be answered, each for himself, is the one propounded by the Roman governor of Jerusalem, "What shall I do then with Jesus, which is called Christ!" (Matt. xxvii. 22).

Copyright © 2024 by Alicia EDITIONS
Credits: www.canva.com; Alicia EDITIONS,
PAPERBACK: 9782384552719
E-BOOK: 9782384552726
HARDCOVER: 9782384552733
All rights reserved.
No part of this book may be reproduced in any form or by any electronic or mechanical means, including information storage and retrieval systems, without written permission from the author, except for the use of brief quotations in a book review.

www.ingramcontent.com/pod-product-compliance
Lightning Source LLC
LaVergne TN
LVHW032012070526
838202LV00059B/6406